The Writer's ABC Checklist

Lorraine Mace
and
Maureen Vincent-Northam

Published by Accent Press Ltd – 2010

ISBN 9781907016196

Printed and bound in the UK
by CPI Bookmarque, Croydon, CR0 4TD

Cover design by Red Dot Design

Dedication

Because writing is a lone occupation, requiring both sacrifice and understanding from family, we would like to thank our husbands.

To Chris, my husband and best friend, for his love and endless support.
Maureen

For Derek, with love and thanks for always being there – my number one fan.
Lorraine

Acknowledgements

We would like to thank the many people who have asked us writing-related questions over the years. The inspiration for *The Writer's ABC Checklist* came from each and every one of you.

We also wish to thank Accent Press for their belief in our book.

Table of Contents

Preface

As most writers know, there is something extremely daunting about putting together a submission. Indeed, even established writers worry about presenting their work so that it makes the right impression. Whether it is an idea for an article, a short story for a magazine, a humorous anecdote, a novel or a non-fiction book, it is essential to present the work in such a way that the editors or publishers will feel they are being approached by a professional.

Will your work make the grade, or is your presentation letting you down? Poor presentation singles the writer out as an amateur, which can mean your work being rejected before it has been read. In a busy editor's office they receive so many manuscripts that they actively look for reasons to reject work. So what is the best way to avoid your efforts landing in the instant rejection pile?

Asking for a publication's guidelines is only the beginning of the process. What is it the editor actually wants? How should the manuscript be laid out? Double or single line spacing? What do the guidelines mean by synopsis? What should be in a covering letter and when should one be included? What is a title page? Whatever form your writing takes, this book provides the answers to all your questions, including those you didn't even know you should ask.

The A-Z format means the answers to specific questions can be found quickly and effortlessly. A quick glance through the index of this easy-to-follow guide shows where to go to learn the tricks of the trade which will get your work noticed for all the right reasons.

Where appropriate, the sections are carefully cross-referenced. This ensures that unfamiliar terms are explained. The references also point to the next logical step in the submission process. You can be happy in the knowledge that every angle has been covered and your submission will not declare you an amateur.

Bullet points are included at the end of most sections, providing a quick reminder of the main items covered.

This book will not teach you how to write (there are several excellent books on the market for that purpose and we have included a suggested list of further reading material). Our aim is to give you the best possible chance of seeing your writing published.

This is, quite simply, the ultimate guide to professional presentation. This unique book is packed with writing tips and is something no aspiring writer can afford to be without.

A

Abbreviations

See also: *Capital Letters, Final Checks, House Style, Proofreading*

Abbreviations are used all the time to shorten the names of organisations and technical terms so that they're easier to remember. These are most often sets of initials, but what is the correct way to write them down?

There are a number of conventional rules for abbreviations and many publications have their own preference. But if this isn't immediately apparent to you, choose one of the accepted customs and stick to it throughout your work – above all, be consistent.

Some abbreviations are so commonly used they need no further clarification: NHS, for example. But usually the longer name is used in full at the first mention, followed by the abbreviation in brackets: National Health Service (NHS). You need only write the abbreviation from then on. If you are using the name of an organisation only once in your article there is no need to supply an abbreviation for it.

When submitting to an overseas title, it is advisable to write out commonly used names in full when used for the first time.

If an abbreviation is unfamiliar, or looks awkward when written repeatedly, try using a generic word in its place such as the group, the corporation, or the organisation.

When writing with publication in mind, some commonly used abbreviations should be avoided and instead the full words substituted: use 'that is' rather than i.e., use 'for example' rather than e.g.

Abbreviations can be written using or omitting full stops, though it is becoming more usual in creative writing to leave them out. For example, most people use BBC rather than B.B.C. and UK rather than U.K. The same rule applies to names, Mr J T Smith now being more frequently used than Mr. J. T. Smith.

It is usual to include a full stop at the end of a contraction where the first letters are written and the rest of the word is omitted. For example, Rev. for Reverend or Prof. for Professor.

But where an abbreviation includes the last letter as well as the first, you do not take a full stop. For example, Dr for Doctor or Ltd for Limited.

Use only one full stop if your sentence ends with an abbreviation that already includes full stops.

When an original word is capitalised, the abbreviated word always retains its capital letter. For example, United Kingdom becomes UK. For words normally spelt with lower case letters, there is no hard and fast rule: POV or pov for point of view are both correct.

A lower case s, without an apostrophe, is added to an abbreviation to indicate a plural: TVs, CDs, MPs, and so on. And an apostrophe is not needed to indicate a shortened word when it has become a recognised word in its own right. So use phone not 'phone, use plane not 'plane.

To summarise:
- Be consistent
- Write full name followed by initials after first use
- Write common names in full for overseas publications
- Avoid abbreviations in creative writing

Accrediting Sources

See also: Acquiring Rights, Articles, Legal, Newspapers, Quotes, Research

The careful assembling of facts (see also *Research*) will lend authority to your work. To an editor it is an indication of the 'behind the scenes' research undertaken by you in order to make your article or book as accurate as possible.

The editor will want to know the origin of your material, how reliable the facts are and whether they came from an authoritative source. Therefore, any data you may have gathered from another author's work or from an original document should be acknowledged.

Information judged to be common knowledge does not have to be accredited. Stating in your article that Antananarivo is the capital city of Madagascar would be considered common knowledge, even if you did need to look up the information. But you should accredit your source when citing a lesser-known fact about the country, or something which could be disputed – the ratio of males to females, or the country's most popular family pastime, for example. If you are in any doubt about something being common knowledge, always accredit your source.

Keep detailed notes of your sources in a file on your computer or in a notebook as you track them down; this will save you heaps of time when you come to compile a list of references for your manuscript – never just trust this to memory.

When submitting an article to a magazine use a separate sheet of paper to list all the sources you have used in your research and head it Sources or References.

If you gathered your information from several sources,

you may need to subdivide the page: Books, Original documents, Magazines, Internet and so on.

Within each section, list your sources in alphabetical order by the authors' surnames. You will need to give relevant information about each resource you have used.

The following is the generally accepted method used by most magazine editors:

Books:

Author's surname, author's first name. Title of the book. Place of publication. Name of publisher. Date published. Page number.

Magazines:

Author's surname, author's first name. Title of the article. Title of the publication. Full date of publication. Page number.

Original documents:

Title of the document. Collection name. Date written or recorded. File or document number. Location of repository.

Internet:

Author's surname, author's first name. Title of the article. Website address. Date published.

The Harvard System:

If you are writing a more academic piece – an essay, for example – you may be required to cite your references using the Harvard System. This is also known as the author-date system. Individual schools and universities will instruct you in their preferred method, but here is a simplified example of how the Harvard System works.

When citing a reference, the author's surname and the publication year are inserted into the text in the relevant place.

Example:

"According to Robinson (2006), children become

embroiled in the already difficult issue of separation."

The author's surname and date of publication will be inserted each time you make a reference to this particular work. At the end of your document, the complete reference must be cited and should include: author name, date of publication, title of book, where published and publisher's name. These will be listed in alphabetical order by author surname.

Example:

Robinson, M (2006). The Custody Minefield. United Kingdom. Orana Publishing Ltd

Whichever system of referencing you use, the most important thing is to be consistent in your choice throughout.

To summarise:

- Acknowledge the data you've used from another author's work
- Accredit the source when using facts not considered common knowledge
- Keep a record of your sources – never trust to memory

Acquiring Rights

See also: Accrediting Sources, Legal, Quotes

If a writer uses a direct extract from a song, dialogue from a film, or any other published work, it is necessary to obtain the permission of the copyright holder. There are exceptions (fair use), but these exceptions are limited and only apply in certain clearly defined circumstances.

Fair use allows the inclusion of names and titles without permission and can also incorporate short extracts, but what constitutes a short extract is a hazy concept and, if in any doubt, it is advisable to obtain permission. For more information about fair use and using extracts from copyright material visit the UK Copyright Service at www.copyrightservice.co.uk.

If the work you wish to use is not in the public domain, the first organisation to contact is the publisher. Most publishers have departments that deal with permissions and will be able to advise whom to contact if they do not hold the rights themselves.

Where the author of the work is known to you personally, it is advisable to get a written agreement covering use to avoid possible problems at a future date.

If you wish to use passages from a website, and the website author's details are not available, then contact the Webmaster. If using images to illustrate your work the permission of the photographer must be obtained.

You must obtain any necessary permissions prior to the publication of your own work. In most cases, a fee will be involved and a licence will be granted specifying the exact circumstances under which the work may be used.

You must always include the source of the material, the name of the owner and the correct copyright notice.

To summarise:

- Obtain consent from the relevant copyright holder
- Get a written agreement before using another's work
- Gain permission *before* you publish your work

Agents – When and How to Approach Them

See also: Books, Children's Picture Books, Covering Letters, Fiction, Teen Fiction, Yours Sincerely

Plenty of authors have sold their books directly to a publisher, but there are a number of benefits in acquiring the services of an agent.

Agents are well informed about market trends, able to assess your work and offer it to the most suitable publisher. They will advise, check over your publishing contract and negotiate the best terms on your behalf.

So when is the right time to approach an agent and how do you go about it?

Not surprisingly, the most advantageous time to approach an agent is when a publisher shows an interest in your book – but before you sign a publishing contract.

Finding an agent:

Make a list of the agents you want to contact. Those who handle the type of book you have written, or are in the process of writing, are the ones to aim at. This can be done in a number of ways.

- Look in the acknowledgements sections of books in your chosen genre; the author often thanks a helpful agent
- *The Bookseller,* a weekly publication, gives key information about the book industry and often carries news about which agents have sold new books – make a note of the ones who seem to be handling books like yours
- Check the listings in the *Writers' and Artists' Yearbook* and *The Writer's Handbook*
- Attend writers' conferences where agents are booked as guest speakers

The approach:

Each agent has his or her preferred method of approach. A large number now have websites and some will accept submissions by email, but do check individual guidelines for exact requirements.

Many agents do not accept unsolicited manuscripts and prefer a query letter in the first instance. If an agent doesn't have a website, write to those on your list asking if you may submit work, enclosing a stamped addressed envelope for a reply. Ask the agent to confirm the submission requirements as these differ – some may want to see a detailed proposal, while others will also request a given number of chapters.

Your preliminary letter should be clear and to the point. Explain why there is a need for your book and how the book meets that need. Mention any specific qualifications you have for writing your book and whether you can supply photographs to illustrate it.

Tell the agent that you intend to send your full book proposal to one agent at a time and invite him to contact you as soon as possible if he is interested. If you receive a favourable reply to your preliminary letter, mail your book proposal (and chapters if these were requested), enclosing return postage.

Sending your book proposal:

Submit your book proposal and chapters to one agent at a time, even if more than one responded to your initial query. Your cover letter should reiterate the fact that this is an exclusive submission. On the envelope write 'Requested material' so the office knows this is not unsolicited work.

If you haven't heard from the agent within three months, you may wish to send your book proposal out to another agent who has shown an interest. Send a polite letter to the first agent explaining this, giving her the opportunity of contacting you if she is interested in your proposal.

If you hear nothing, send to the next agent on your list. An agent who rejects your proposal may sometimes tell you what he didn't like about it. This professional advice can be very useful; it may help you to improve your work by incorporating some of the new ideas.

Some publishers will only agree to look at work

submitted by agents, knowing this work will be of a high standard, but it can be harder to find an agent than a publisher.

To summarise:

- Aim only at those agents who handle books in your field
- Send a preliminary letter in the first instance
- Submit your proposal to one agent at a time
- Take note of any professional advice an agent offers

Angles – Old Ideas with a New Perspective

See also: *Anniversary Pitches, Fiction, Hooks, Photography, Queries, Research, Teen Fiction, Topics*

A good article requires meticulous research, which is very time consuming. However, facts garnered for one piece can be utilised for several different publications as long as a unique perspective is used with each submission.

For example, research on a major figure, such as Lord Nelson, will bring to light numerous possible avenues to explore. His life with Emma Hamilton, his naval career, Trafalgar, the ships associated with his famous battles, life in Britain during that period, Napoleon Bonaparte, the Napoleonic Wars, and many more topics. From this list, you can see that the information is too wide for one article, but, if you think laterally, it's possible to use the information to query several different titles. Always look at your research in the widest possible sense and never limit yourself to one sale per subject.

Articles and reviews already published, or pieces written 'on spec' but not taken up by the intended market, can be rewritten and presented in a different format. Use bits of several different pieces to create an entirely new (and saleable) article. The important point when using existing ideas is to present them in a new and interesting way.

Try to look at your ideas from a different perspective. Remember that editors receive numerous queries each day and yours has to stand out. Writing about coastal erosion, although interesting in its own right, is more likely to grab an editor's eye if a personal aspect is added. An interview with someone whose home is threatened by coastal erosion, or who has had to move as a result, turns it into a human interest feature.

Illustrating an article gives an added dimension and will often mean the difference between the editor saying yes or no to your idea. Look at your photographs and see if one of them suggests a different slant that you could use to make your piece fresh and original.

To summarise:
- Utilise your research to cover more angles
- Refocus several articles to create an entirely new one
- Look for unique ways to write about your subject
- Add a human interest slant if you can

Anniversary Pitches

See also: *Angles, Articles, Discipline – Staying on Topic, Markets, Queries*

An anniversary article is one of the easiest, but also one of the hardest, to sell. Easy because editors are always on the lookout for interesting anniversary features, but hard because you have to come up with a reason why yours should be the pitch that wins the day. Remember, if you know it is an important anniversary, so do many other writers who will also be aiming to sell their idea.

Try to look at the personality and/or event from every possible point of view. Doing this not only makes you think of different ways of dealing with the anniversary, it also gives more market choices. Using the same research to create several different queries, which can then be sent to various publications, will multiply your success rate.

Timing, when sending queries to editors, is crucial for anniversary article proposals. For weekly magazines the idea should be on the editor's desk at least three months prior to the anniversary date, preferably six months ahead if possible. For monthly magazines six months is the absolute minimum, nine months ahead is better. This may seem an unreasonably long lead time, but remember that most monthly magazines are published a month in advance of the cover date, the theme having been decided up to a year earlier. The sooner you can put your anniversary proposal together, the better your chances of a commission.

Your target publications for an article featuring an anniversary can range from general interest (such as *The Lady* and *Ireland's Own*) to trade, country, county, specialist and newspaper supplement magazines. If the anniversary is local to your area it is highly likely that regional newspapers would also be interested.

To summarise:
- Look at the personality, or event, from various points of view
- Send in your proposal well ahead of time
- Consider local publications as well as national ones

Articles – Checking the Structure

See also: Angles, Anniversary Pitches, Discipline – Staying on Topic, Fillers, Final Checks, Guidelines, Hooks, Jargon and Slang, Markets, Newspapers, Opinion Pieces, Outlines, Photography, Queries, Research, Serial Rights, Sidebars, Travel Writing

A great deal of thought should be given to the way an article is structured. The theme determined, the facts gathered and sorted into a logical sequence, the punch line decided for a humour piece and the length divided into three important sections. These sections should then be looked at individually to give the greatest impact to the article as a whole.

The opening paragraph:

The way a writer deals with the opening paragraph of an article is crucial. If you haven't grabbed your readers with the first few sentences, it is highly unlikely they will bother to read on. Bearing in mind that the first reader is the editor who will be deciding whether or not to run it, this highlights how vital it is to get it exactly right.

From the opening paragraph the reader should be able to grasp what the article is about and also have gleaned enough information to want to find out more. It should ask questions, present startling or unusual facts, tease, amuse or astound – but, above all, it should draw the reader in to the rest of the story.

The main body:

The facts should be presented in a clear, easy-to-read format, the language being tailored to suit the target publication's readers. The use of jargon should be kept to an absolute minimum (and avoided altogether if at all possible).

The information used must be relevant and the original focus not obscured by unnecessary facts. Most important of all though, is that it should be interesting to read.

The tone of the article must be suited to both the subject matter and the target publication. Humour should only be used where appropriate.

The closing paragraph:

A good closing paragraph summarises what has gone before and often refers back to the opening paragraph. It should tie up any loose ends and leave the reader feeling satisfied with the article as a whole. If a humour piece, the punch line should fit the rest of the article and not seem contrived.

To summarise:

- Grab your reader's attention in the opening paragraph
- Write in a tone that suits your target market
- Use your closing paragraph to tie up loose ends

B

Biography – Writing a Short Author's Bio
See also: Clips, Press Release

An author's bio, the brief biography which sometimes follows a published story or article, need be no longer than a few sentences. It cites an author's relevant knowledge, interest, or credentials for writing a particular piece.

A bio should always be written in the third person and tailored to suit the market for which you are writing. Although there's no need to list every one individually, it is a good idea to mention any previous writing credits. You could also list any qualifications you have regarding your chosen subject, or any former experience writing in the same field.

For example:

Mary Smith is a member of the National Institute of Medical Herbalists. She has written articles for several natural health publications and writes a regular column for *Herbs and Health* magazine.

If you have credits, but they don't include the subject you are writing about, your bio might look something like this:

Mary Smith's stories and articles have been published in the UK and France. She is a natural health enthusiast and has read widely on women's central role in herbal medicine.

And if you don't yet have any writing credits?

Mary Smith lives in London with her husband and three children. She has had a life-long interest in natural medicine and she puts her family's good health down to a sensible diet and simple herbal remedies.

To summarise:
- Write in the third person
- Tailor your bio to suit the publication you are writing for
- Mention any pertinent credits

Books

See also: *Agents, Children's Picture Books, Dialogue, Fiction, Guidelines, Publishers, Serial Rights, Synopsis, Teen Fiction, Vanity Publishers, Word Count*

Researching the market
Fiction:

There are many different types of novels but the chances are, for a first novel, you will have chosen to write yours in a genre that also appeals to you as a reader: fantasy, romance, family saga, horror, whodunit, and so on.

It's always advisable to read widely in your chosen genre but, even more importantly, read books which are being published now and analyse them carefully. This will ensure that you are aware of current conventions regarding style, length and content. Emulate these practices in your own novel, but aim to provide something new – publishers aren't interested in carbon copies of other works.

Book lengths vary enormously; most novels are between 75,000 and 95,000 words, some others – regional sagas and fantasy, for example – reach double that figure. The average children's full-length novel is usually between 30,000 and 45,000 words.

Most publishers have websites and many include online guidelines regarding required book length. Publishers' submission guidelines will indicate how many sample chapters they want to see – usually between one and four

– and whether they want the opening chapters.

Non-fiction:

It's important to have a specific readership in mind when planning a non-fiction book. Whom do you visualise reading your book and what will they gain from it? There will almost certainly be other books on the same topic, so how will yours stand out from the rest? Will it encompass new research, be better, more in-depth, or deal with an area not covered elsewhere?

Whether or not a publisher is familiar with your topic, he will expect you to identify any competing titles. Before commissioning your non-fiction book he will want a clear idea of any similar books available, their target readership, what each of those titles try to do and how yours would fit into the current market. For the best chance of success, study other books that have been written on your subject and look for a gap in the market, which your book could fill.

Your objective is to sell the idea before you write the book. This makes sense for a number of reasons: a publisher may be interested in the book's concept, but only take it on if it's written in a specific format to complement an existing series; he might want the book longer or shorter, or ask you to write it from a slightly different angle.

Choosing the right publisher

Market research is important when looking for a suitable publisher as no publishing house takes on every kind of book. It would be pointless sending your non-fiction manuscript to a publisher who handles only fiction, or submitting your historical romance to one interested only in educational books.

Study the listings in the *Writers' & Artists' Yearbook* and *The Writer's Handbook* and submit your manuscript only to those who commission books in your chosen genre.

Published weekly, another very useful resource to study is *The Bookseller* magazine. It contains up-to-date information on publishers and their recent acquisitions and could identify those handling similar novels to yours, or highlight any gaps in the market that your non-fiction book might fill. Their Spring and Autumn Buyer's Guides and the Children's Buyer's Guides review thousands of forthcoming books.

Some publishers have book 'series' and you might find your non-fiction book would fit the remit of an existing series. These books are usually written to a specific format with regard to length and style and cover themes such as 'how-to' books.

It's also a good idea to check out publishers' websites as these usually have catalogues listing the books they publish. A little investigating on your part will tell you what books are currently selling in bookstores, their focus, length and, most importantly, who publishes them.

To summarise:

- Research the market by reading similar works that are published now
- Plan your non-fiction book with a specific readership in mind
- Fill a gap in the market
- Submit only to publishers who handle books in your chosen genre

C

Capital Letters

See also: Abbreviations, Proofreading, Quotes

Capital letters are often used incorrectly. We all know they come at the start of a sentence, but other uses include names of people, places, events, quotes, abbreviations and titles.

Names

The pronoun 'I' always has a capital letter. As well as names like John Smith or Mary Jones, capitals are needed when used in place of proper nouns for family names such as Mum, Dad, Granddad, Aunt, and also for titles such as Inspector and so on. For all other purposes these nouns are not capitalised.

Shall we meet for lunch, Mum?

I met my mum for lunch today.

I'll try to answer your questions, Inspector.

The inspector asked me some tricky questions.

People's titles should always have capital letters.

Prime Minister, Prince Charles, Sir Edward Elgar.

But when using *sir* and *madam* as courtesy titles only they are not capitalised.

The dog ate my homework, sir.

Are you being served, madam?

Buildings, institutions and organisations only need a capital letter when it forms part of a specific name, but not when it appears on its own.

My son attends Whitecross High School.

I'll be going to high school next term.

I put all my money in Trustus Building Society.

What time does the building society open?

In the titles of books, films, plays, magazines, newspapers and pieces of music, a capital letter is generally used for the start of the first word and for each key word, but is not necessary for words like *and*, *the*, *to*, *in*, *of* and so on.

Lost for Words

Angels and Demons

News of the World

Place names such as South Africa or Northern Ireland are capitalised, but when simply denoting a geographical area no capital is used – southern Spain, northern France. A capital letter is used for adjectives such as African, Irish, Spanish and French. The exception to this is when the connection is distant and does not necessarily refer to the place, for example, danish pastry, french windows, yorkshire pudding or brussels sprouts.

Manufacturers and brand-named products are capitalised.

Sony PlayStation

Ford Ka

Hoover

Sellotape

Some brand names have become so much a part of our everyday speech that no capital is used.

I had just finished hoovering the carpet.

I'm going to sellotape this envelope down.

Numbering

Roman numerals are usually capitalised: MMIX, XIV, IIV. The general exception is when they are used to number the prelim pages in books.

Quotes

The first word of a direct quotation – repeating someone else's exact words – is always capitalised if the quotation is a complete sentence.

Bob Hope famously quipped, "Middle age is when your age starts to show around your middle."

No capital letter is used if the quotation is not a complete sentence.

Inspector Brown described his latest case as "baffling".

Time periods

Capital letters are used for days of the week and months of the year. They are not needed for seasons or for the points of the compass: spring, south

Historical periods are also capitalised: Gothic, the Renaissance, the Depression, the Middle Ages.

To summarise:

Capitals needed for:

- The pronoun 'I'
- A proper name
- A person's title
- The first and key words in the title of a book, etc
- The name of a country and language
- A brand name
- The name of a day or a month
- The name of a historical period
- A Roman numeral
- The first word of a direct quotation

Children's Picture Books

See also: *Fiction, Guidelines, Illustrations, Layout and Formatting, Publishers, Serial Rights*

For most children's books, the layout is the same as for adult books. Picture books, which are highly illustrated story books designed to be read aloud to the very young, are an exception. Because the storylines are both simple and fun, picture books are a popular choice for those who want to write for children.

These books have short, uncomplicated sentences with an easy rhythm and a certain amount of repetition in the text, particularly of the characters' names. They do, in fact, look simple to write, but this is deceptive – picture books are amongst the hardest to write and to sell.

If you study the market you will notice that picture books are written in a very different way to books aimed at older children. There is no need for descriptive passages in order to set the scene; the illustrator will do that with her artwork. The illustrations have a major role to play in telling the story, filling in the necessary details which the text leaves out.

Although you don't have to provide the pictures yourself, you do need to visualise them as you create your story because the placement of your words with these imaginary illustrations will be a key factor in the layout of your manuscript.

The majority of picture books have thirty-two pages. Other lengths are published, but the number of pages is always divisible by eight – twenty-four, forty, and sixty-four. You will in fact have eight pages fewer than this to work with. For a thirty-two page picture book for example, you will only have twenty-four pages on which to tell your story. Here's why:

- The outer front and back covers are counted as page one and page thirty-two
- The inside of the front and back covers are pages two and thirty-one
- Page three and page thirty are always blank sheets
- Page four is the title page
- Page five contains the publisher's details, copyright information and ISBN number

This means your story will begin on page 6 and finish on

page 29.

Example of layout:

Use double spacing on white A4 paper.

Page 6:   Timmy's brother is very little.

Page 7:   He has little fingers, little toes, little ears, and a little nose.

Page 8:   But Timmy's little brother has a very BIG voice.

Page 9:   When he yells, he makes a very LOUD noise. He wakes the dog. He scares the cat. And he makes the windows rattle.

To summarise:

- Sentences should be short and uncomplicated
- Illustrations enhance the text by filling in detail
- Visualise the pictures as you write
- Most picture books have thirty-two pages

Clichés

See also: Consistency, Dialogue, Final Checks, Originality, X Factor

Whether writing fiction or non-fiction, clichés are a writer's worst enemy. They scream amateur louder than any other mistake a writer might make. A manuscript liberally sprinkled with clichés will often be discarded after the first page has been read – always assuming the editor, publisher, or agent, gets that far.

What is a cliché?

The *Concise Oxford Dictionary* defines it as a hackneyed phrase or opinion, and, from a writer's point of view, it shows not only lack of originality, but also inexperience.

Non-fiction:

When wishing to convey a sense of atmosphere or

describe scenery, as for a travel article, try to avoid the obvious. The blood-red sunset or sunrise has risen and set so many times, it's a wonder the sun bothers to get up at all. Canyons may well be grandiose, awe-inspiring, breath-taking or incredible, but do remember editors have seen those words thousands of times before. Your canyons needn't be any bigger or better, but your descriptions need to be original and fresh.

Similarly, sleazy politicians, drug-addicted musicians, warm-hearted dinner ladies and over-worked doctors are descriptions that have appeared so often, they are almost part of the job criteria. Why should an editor pay for something that has been written over and over again?

Fiction:

In fiction there are even more pitfalls waiting to catch the inexperienced writer. Characterisation, narrative and dialogue are all places where your writing could be clichéd and devoid of originality.

Heroines are not always beautiful; heroes can be flawed. Avoid steely gazes, smouldering glances, sultry sirens and other such overworked drivel, or you might just as well stamp the word 'beginner' on the first page of your manuscript.

In the narrative, don't use stereotypical phrases. A private detective's office needn't be dingy; the city executive doesn't have to have a palatial office suite. Make sure you bring your imagination into every aspect of your work.

Dialogue is the one area where clichés can work for you. Although they should be avoided in general, when used to define one character in particular, they can be very effective. But, as with everything else, use common sense when you have characters using cliché-ridden dialogue and don't overdo it. Have them using enough to be easily identified by their speech, but not so much that it is no longer believable.

To summarise:

- Editors can spot a cliché a mile away (that's an example of clichéd writing)
- Originality of thought and prose is essential
- Find new ways to describe settings and atmosphere
- Clichéd dialogue can be used to define a character

Clips

See also: *Editors, Markets, Queries, Websites and Blogs*

Clips are photocopied samples of previously published work and are used by editors to appraise your writing ability.

A magazine editor will sometimes require clips when you ask him about an article idea. They will verify that you've been published before and show him that you are capable of writing for his publication.

Where possible, you should send samples that are relevant to the topic you are proposing. If you don't have clips relating to the subject in hand, send two or three samples of your best work.

But what if you have no clips? Will this jeopardise your chances of getting the assignment? Not always, as not every publication asks for them, especially the smaller or lower-paying ones – these markets will often agree to look at work 'on spec'.

Writing for the smaller markets – which are not so swamped with queries – is where a new writer can build up a useful portfolio of published writing samples.

Local daily and weekly newspapers need a lot of copy to fill their pages and frequently accept work from freelance writers.

Many businesses produce a trade magazine and will consider articles pertinent to their company, while clubs and societies publish newsletters and often welcome an approach.

These are low, or non-paying, markets, but can help build a valuable collection of writing clips.

Photocopy the original printed piece and mark it with the name of the publication and the date it was published.

Giving editors the link to a personal website where your writing is showcased is another way of presenting clips; this works particularly well when querying an online market.

To summarise:

- Send clips relevant to the topic you are proposing
- Write for smaller publications in order to gain writing samples
- Mark your clips with date and details of when published

Competitions

See also: *Layout and Formatting, Title Page, Word Count*

Before pressing 'send' on the computer, or dropping the envelope containing a competition entry in the post box, there are certain questions all writers should ask themselves.

As with any writing endeavour, checking the market is of paramount importance to stand the best chance of success. You may not think it is possible to do very much market research for a competition, but in fact, it is fairly easy to make sure your entry fulfils the judge's criteria.

Judges

Find out who the judges are and run an Internet search on them. Visit their websites and read as many of their own works of fiction as you can. This will give you a good idea of the type of writing and style that appeals to them.

Manuscript

Most competitions require the story to be typed with double spacing and using one side of the page only. If in doubt, check with the competition organisers, although this information is usually found in the rules.

If sending an email entry, make sure you are using the format the organisers have stipulated. If they say no attachments, they mean exactly that and will normally delete any attachments unread.

Never put your details on the actual story. Attach a title page giving your name, address, email address, telephone number, the story's title and word count.

Number the pages and make sure the title appears in the top right-hand corner of every page. Put more follows, mf, more, or m/f, in the bottom right-hand corner of every page except for the last. On the last page at the end of the story type The End.

Rules

The rules of a competition are rigid and must be adhered to completely. If the word count is set at 1,000 words, do not write one word more. Check to see if the title has to be included in the word count – this varies, so should always be verified.

The closing date given for entries is never flexible. Don't imagine that your story is so wonderful the judges will overlook the fact it arrived a day late – they won't. If the submission must be postmarked, received in the competition headquarters, or emailed, before a certain date, then it is up to you to make sure your entry arrives in plenty of time.

Style

Maintain your own style, but not at the expense of ruining your chances. If the competition theme and the judge's own works point to romance, a hard-edged crime with lots of violence is not likely to find favour. Read previous winning stories to find out what it is that the competition organisers are looking for.

Theme

Many competitions are open-themed, but where a theme has been specified you must write to it. Be original in your take on the subject by all means, the more original the better, but you must stay within the remit laid down.

To summarise:

- Read and follow the rules without deviation
- Stay within the word count
- Submit within the deadline period
- Be original, but do not stray outside the theme
- Read the judge's own fiction
- Do not put your name on the actual story pages
- Number the pages and put the title on each page

Computers

See also: Layout and Formatting, Letterheads, Markets, Typing, Word Count

Microsoft Word is the word processing programme favoured by most writers and editors. Written in Word, and saved as a Word document, your manuscript will be compatible with the systems used by the majority of publications and therefore more acceptable to them.

There are many handy tools in Word that can make life

easier for you and add a professional look to your manuscript.

Auto-correct

Most of us find we misspell certain words time after time. When this happens, the quick solution is to correct your misspelling in the AutoCorrect feature.

Right-click on the misspelled word and a menu will appear. If alternative spellings are offered in the menu, there will also be a menu choice called AutoCorrect. Choose this and you will be shown the same spelling alternatives in a submenu. Select the correct spelling from this list. Now each time you misspell that word, it will automatically be corrected.

Find and replace

This makes it possible to change a word or phrase within your manuscript automatically, without the need to trawl through the whole document – very useful if you decide to change a character's name, for instance.

Position your cursor at a point in your manuscript. Choose Find from the Edit menu. Select 'Replace' in the window that opens and type in the word or phrase you'd like to change in the 'Find what' box. Next type in the word or phrase you'd like to replace it in the 'Replace with' box. Select the 'All' option if you want to make changes to the whole document; alternatively choose 'Up' or 'Down' if you want the changes above or below the cursor.

You can choose to alter words and phrases manually by clicking the 'Find Next' or 'Replace' buttons, or select 'Replace All' for this to be done automatically.

Do take care when using 'Replace All' to make multiple changes to your manuscript, making sure that what is in the 'Replace' box is *exactly* what is required, e.g. that there are no surplus leading or trailing spaces.

Language

The settings can be adjusted by choosing Language from the Tools menu so that your document will check spellings in other languages. This is especially helpful if you intend to submit your manuscript to an overseas market. It will, for example, differentiate between UK and US English.

Quick clicks

- To select a word, position the cursor within the word and double-click

- To select a line, position the cursor in the left-hand margin so that it becomes an arrow and then point at the line you wish to highlight and click

- To select a complete paragraph, position the cursor anywhere within the paragraph and triple-click

- To select a sentence, hold down the CTRL key as you click anywhere within the sentence

Spelling and grammar check

Set the spelling and grammar check to look for errors in your work automatically by choosing Options from the Tools menu, then selecting the spelling and grammar tab and set to check automatically. This being in place, an incorrect spelling will be underlined in red and questionable grammar underlined in green.

What the spell checker won't highlight are words that are spelt correctly, but used in the wrong context: for example, it won't find 'stationary' where you should have used 'stationery', or 'pore' where 'pour' would have been correct. Because of this, it's vital that you don't rely on the spell checker alone – always read your work through to spot any errors the checker has missed.

Although the grammar check is useful as a general guide, be aware that it isn't always correct and will sometimes suggest options that turn your sentences into gobbledygook.

Thesaurus

This can be found by choosing Language from the Tools menu and then Thesaurus from the submenu or by inserting the cursor in the word you wish to check and pressing SHIFT+F7. A list of synonyms is accessible by right-clicking on a word.

Word count

An accurate word count of your manuscript can be done by placing the cursor anywhere in the document and choosing Word Count from the Tools menu. Alternatively, if you wish to check the word count of only part of the document, highlight the text you wish to calculate before choosing Word Count from the Tools menu.

To summarise:

- Use the spelling and grammar checker, but read your work, too
- AutoCorrect frequently misspelled words
- Reset the Language feature to match that of an overseas market

Consistency

See also: Computers, Continuity, Dates, Dialogue, Final Checks, Foreign Words and Phrases, House Style, Layout and Formatting, Notebooks, Point of View, Proofreading, Research, Tense, ZZZZ – Sleep on It

Whatever form your writing takes, consistency should be your watchword. Whether fact or fiction, it is essential that you check, check and check again to confirm you have maintained uniformity in every aspect of your writing.

Ensure that the layout of your manuscript is unvarying from beginning to end. Don't have page numbers at the top on some pages and at the bottom on others. Are your margins and tabs the same throughout the document? Is the line spacing consistent? If you began with headings in bold using a particular font and size, have you continued in the same way?

Non-fiction:

Choose a particular style of writing and stick with it. Don't start an article in a relaxed, chatty manner only for your writing to become formal midway through the piece. Similarly, if the market calls for a more restrained style, that should be maintained throughout.

If using foreign words, make sure they have all been placed in italics. Titles of published works, films, television programmes and suchlike should also appear in italics throughout.

Fiction:

For fiction, it is essential to ensure you have maintained point of view and not switched mid-scene. In the following example the scene has been set from George's point of view.

Wrong: George was worried, it was all going wrong. Max thought George was weak.

Right: George was worried, it was all going wrong. He knew Max thought he was weak.

Dialogue marks – check that you've used either single or double, but not a mixture of the two. The exception to this is when using one inside the other to denote speech within speech, as per example on page 83.

Character traits

Dialogue very often establishes characteristics more effectively than using narrative, but this can be lost if your character isn't consistent in his manner of speech.

If he starts with dialogue peppered with slang on page one, he'd better still be doing so on the last page, unless the novel is about his transformation.

Having established your fictional cast, don't let them do things that are out of character, unless you can make it believable. Someone scared of the dark at the beginning is not going to willingly venture into a gloomy forest, but he might if his life, or that of a loved one, depended on it.

Dialect

Using dialect for your characters – regional accents and inflections, or irregular pronunciation and terminology – can easily be overdone, and having to wade through pages of deliberately misspelled words can defeat even the keenest reader.

Rather than creating a well-rounded and unique individual, using dialect can make your writing unnecessarily difficult to comprehend. The occasional word or phrase is enough to give a flavour of a character's accent or speech pattern.

Limit your use, but if you do choose a certain spelling to highlight a character's dialect, stick to it throughout your story.

Names

You may decide to change the name of one or more of your characters. If you do, make sure that everything to do with that character is amended. Don't have your heroine in love with Mark on page three and getting married to Matthew on page five, only to be divorcing Mark at the end of the book.

Another common error to watch out for is inconsistent spelling of the same name. Don't let Ann become Anne or Stephen emerge in later chapters as Steven.

Use the search and replace feature on your computer, but

you should also check manually to ensure that none have been missed.

Setting

When setting the scene for your novel, or short fiction, it is important to be consistent. If the novel is set in the fens of Cambridgeshire, the action cannot include any hill climbing. A foreign locale must be rigorously researched before using it as the backdrop for your novel. You'll need to know every aspect of the country and area in order to maintain consistency.

Spelling

Have you checked your spelling? If the work is for the British market, have you used British spelling? American spelling of many common words is very different to that of the UK. Using the wrong type and/or a mixture of both should be avoided.

Weights and measures

Which units of measure did you use at the outset? If using metric at the outset, you cannot switch to Imperial units. Pick one and stick with it, but always make sure the type you use is consistent with the country and era you have used as the setting for your work.

To summarise:

- Choose a style and stick with it
- Check manuscript layout for consistency
- Maintain point of view within scenes
- Check spellings are consistent
- Don't switch between metric and Imperial units

Continuity

See also: Consistency, Fiction, Final Checks, Notebooks, Point of View, Proofreading, Research, Teen Fiction, Tense, ZZZZ – Sleep on It

We've all witnessed those continuity gaffes in movie scenes where the heroine's hair is windswept one moment and neat and sleek the next, or where the hero's side parting switches from the left to the right side and back again.

Writing can be like that, too, so that mistakes in continuity lead to readers' loss of faith in your story's credibility and indignant cries of, 'But that could never have happened!'

Credibility

Ensure your story remains credible. Changing your work by moving blocks of text around the page may improve the general structure of your story, but might alter the logical sequence of events and make nonsense of the continuity.

Plot

Are there any gaping holes in your plot? Does your protagonist set off to work on a Monday morning, only to arrive just in time for a Wednesday afternoon meeting? Did your characters picnic in the June sunshine before gathering blackberries from the hedgerows?

Find out the length of time it takes to get from one destination to another; if someone hops on a train in Edinburgh, she won't be hopping off again at a London station an hour later. Is it possible for someone to cover a distance of five miles on foot in ten minutes? Yet these sorts of mistakes in continuity do occur.

To summarise:

- Be aware of continuity limitations
- Check your plot for feasibility
- Use train timetables and other references to ensure credibility

Covering Letters

See also: *Agents, Editors, Envelopes and sae, Keeping Copies, Letterheads, Publishers, Queries, Typing, Yours Sincerely*

As a matter of courtesy, a covering letter should be included with a magazine article, short story, or book submission. It should include your contact details: mailing address, email and telephone number.

In the case of a magazine article, your covering letter can act as a helpful reminder when you have previously queried an editor with an idea and are now submitting the completed work.

The letter should be business-like and concise – no more than a few paragraphs long. It isn't necessary to describe your article in great detail; refer to it by name and give a brief summary of why the feature will be suitable for this particular publication.

Always write to the magazine's editor, or a specific feature editor, using his or her full name or title (Mr, Ms) and surname.

Look on the editorial page of a recent copy of the magazine in question to find the relevant person to whom you should address your submission. You could also phone the publication's editorial desk for this information, but double check that you have the correct spelling of names.

For a fiction submission, give details of where your fiction has been published in the past. It is not necessary to explain the plot of the story, but you should give the title and the word count.

To summarise:
- Include all your contact details

- Keep your letter brief and business-like
- Address the editor by name and ensure it is spelt correctly

D

Dates

See also: Consistency, Final Checks, Guidelines, House Style, Numbers, Sidebars

As with other writing conventions, it is always best to use a magazine's house style guide when writing dates in an article, but, if this is not available, the following rules will be acceptable in most cases.

Writing dates out in full:

- Omit commas and do not use abbreviations denoting ordinal numbers (st, nd, rd, th)
- 12 March 1958 or 19 June 2006 and not March 12, 1958 or 19th June, 2006

If the day of the week is included:

- Insert a comma after the day – Sunday, 12 August 1955

Only abbreviate the month for information panels (sidebars):

- In the body of the text: 18 September
- In a sidebar: 18 Sept

The general rule is to use capitals for AD and BC. Place AD before the date and BC after:

- 2,600 BC, 15,000 BC
- AD 420–59, AD 55

To give the year of someone's birth or death:

- Use the letter b or d in brackets next to the year (b1925) (d1995)
- When writing both the year of birth and that of death, omit the letters b and d (1925–1995)

Decades:

- 1970s, 1840s or 2000s

- Not: 1970's, 1840's or 2000's

Dialogue

See also: *Fiction, Grammar, Guidelines, Layout and Formatting, Punctuation, Teen Fiction*

Dialogue has to be believable and strong and has to carry the story forward. It should be realistic without including the ums, ers and ahs with which our natural speech is littered. To create character, it is sometimes necessary to include some hesitation in speech pattern, but this should be kept to a minimum.

Each new section of dialogue must be placed on a new line and indented as if it is a new paragraph.

"How could you?" she asked.

"Easily, you drove me to it," he said.

Avoid using adverbs with dialogue tags:

He whispered softly – is there any other way to whisper? She shouted loudly – again, is there any other way to shout?

"Sit there and don't move." That sentence is clearly a command so there is no need to add: she ordered, commanded, or insisted.

Direct speech versus indirect speech

Sometimes, what your character needs to say is too long to use in dialogue (direct speech) and it is better to incorporate some indirect speech.

"What happened in the forest?" he asked and then switched off while Janie went on and on about dragons, werewolves and vampires fighting imaginary battles in a place that didn't exist outside of his daughter's head.

"Wow, that's exciting," he said during one of her all too infrequent pauses for breath.

Imagine how tedious the dialogue would be if Janie

actually narrated the battles. Direct speech takes time, indirect speech shortens the time frame and also gives the reader an insight into the characters' mindset – the father switched off and stopped listening, and the daughter was too excited by the tale to breathe.

Dialogue tags

When characters are involved in a conversation, it isn't necessary to put a dialogue tag after every section of speech. Only use tags when it is unclear who is speaking. The least intrusive of tags is 'said'. Most others stand out and detract from the dialogue.

To see how to punctuate dialogue refer to page 159.

Break it up:

Pages of unbroken dialogue can be tedious to read. Insert sections of narration telling your readers what the characters are doing while all the talking is taking place.

Keep it real:

As a writer, you may want to use dialogue to get vital information across to your reader, but if the words used are not realistic this will fail.

"Thank goodness you've decided to leave John," her mother said – believable dialogue

"Thank goodness you've decided after twenty-five years of abuse by a man with a drinking problem, who beats you every night, and who has been out of work for the last seven years, to leave John," her mother said – unbelievable dialogue

To summarise:

- Keep dialogue believable and use it to move the story forward
- Avoid adverbs where possible
- Switch between direct and indirect speech
- Said is the least intrusive of dialogue tags

- Use narrative to break up large tracts of dialogue
- Don't overuse dialogue to impart back-story

Discipline – Staying on Topic

See also: Articles, Consistency, Continuity, Final Checks, Outlines, Theme

When putting together a non-fiction piece, it's important to keep completely focussed on your chosen subject. An article will immediately lose impact and fail to impress the editor if it begins to depart from the main theme, so chop out any unnecessary pieces of information which have no real bearing on the topic in hand.

To help stay disciplined ask yourself the following questions:

1. Does each sentence relate in some way to the principal topic?
2. Does every paragraph expand the central idea sufficiently?
3. Does the information given in each paragraph follow on in a logical and satisfactory way?

Constructing an outline of your article at the outset will help you to keep on track. List the key points you wish to cover in bold type and arrange them in the order they will appear in your feature. Head each paragraph with one of your key points to ensure you remain disciplined and on topic.

To summarise:

- Keep sharply focussed on your subject
- Cut out unnecessary information
- List the key points your article will cover

E

E-books

See also: Books, Computers, Layout and Formatting, Marketing, Titles

Although any type of manuscript can be published in e-book form, the format is particularly suited to how-to and other non-fiction works. These books aren't long – around 30 pages on average – and contain lively, informative topics that benefit the reader in some way.

Cover

A simple cover design usually works best and gives a more professional look. Choose a photograph, or other image, that symbolises your subject matter, but which doesn't detract from the cover's text. Mixing too many different font styles can look amateurish. A title should be large and bold with a sub-title in smaller type.

An e-book written as a Word document can be converted to a Portable Document Format (PDF) file. This is the industry standard and the most popular software for creating e-books as, once converted, they're tamper-proof and the document itself cannot be altered, or copied, by the reader.

E-books created this way require Adobe Reader to be read, but have the benefit of being accessible to both PC and MAC users.

PDF documents can be produced using Adobe Acrobat software or similar converters which are available as downloads from the Internet. The Adobe website has more information on Portable Document Format:
www.adobe.com/uk.

Graphics and web links

Clipart and photographs can be utilised to great effect,

but use only those which are copyright-free if you aren't the legal copyright holder. Web links should be double-checked to ensure they lead your reader to the intended website.

Layout

E-books are generally read straight from a screen. For ease of reading, create more 'white space' on the page by breaking up the text into shorter paragraphs than might be usual in a printed book, and use generous margins.

As with traditional print books, an e-book will have chapters, sub-headings and a table of contents. The chapters, rather than listed by numbers alone, usually have catchy titles that tell the reader something about the subject matter of that section. Sub-headings will call attention to specific points and make the page more reader-friendly.

Perhaps because e-books are generally considered informal, it is one area of publishing where using coloured text and a less conventional font style is acceptable. Keep in mind reader accessibility; choose a style and colour which complements your topic and stick with it throughout.

To summarise:

- How-to and other non-fiction subjects work best
- For ease of reading, allow plenty of 'white space'
- Font styles and colours should enhance your topic
- A simple cover design has more impact
- For a more professional-looking product, convert into PDF

Edit

See also: *Computers, Consistency, Final Checks,*

Revision and Resubmitting

When you submit stories, or non-fiction articles, to a publication it's vital that your writing is easy to comprehend; a poorly edited piece will result in the reader having to guess at meanings. If an editor has to re-read every other sentence before he can grasp what you're trying to say, it's unlikely he'll even get past the first paragraph or two.

Good editing should have an invisible quality with themes, ideas, and information knitting together effortlessly. Reading your work aloud will identify words that are repeated too frequently and also show up misplaced commas that alter the gist of a sentence.

Awkward phrasing can give your work an entirely different meaning to the one you'd intended.

Examples:

Pupils heard how they could protect themselves from the teacher.

Pupils heard from the teacher how they could protect themselves.

I remember feeding the pigeon in the red dress.

I remember wearing the red dress when I fed the pigeon.

Mary held her headscarf firmly to her head which had a tendency to blow off in the wind.

Mary's headscarf had a tendency to blow off in the wind so she held it firmly to her head.

Look up synonyms to find the word that best describes your ideas. But bear in mind your intended market and the sort of language that publication uses; in most cases straightforward and uncomplicated words are preferred.

Many similar sounding words have very different meanings and create pitfalls for the unwary. If you are in any doubt, look it up in a dictionary.

Examples:
Allude – to hint at or a suggestion of
Elude – to escape, avoid or get away from
Formally – something done in a formal way
Formerly – a previous time
Lightening – to reduce in colour or weight
Lightning – the flash resulting from an electrical storm
Editors can spot well-honed copy at a glance, so careful editing before submitting to your chosen market will greatly increase your chances of acceptance.

To summarise:
- Read your work aloud to highlight any errors
- Check that awkward phrasing hasn't created unintentional bloopers
- Look up the meaning of words you aren't sure about

Editors (Magazines)
See also: The complete index

From the moment you send off your first piece of work you should be thinking in terms of cultivating a relationship with the editor which will be of benefit to both of you. One of the best ways of achieving this is to send work that has been carefully written as a result of extensive market research into the magazine. Your aim should be to know the type of article or fiction the publication runs and write accordingly, incorporating your own original touch. In this way the editor will see you as a professional whose work he wishes to use again and again.

The right approach
Fiction:
The covering letter should be short and simple. If possible, mention other publications that have used your

work, or any competition successes you have achieved. If you are still waiting for your first success, don't say so. You should put in the title of the story and the word count. Include a stamped addressed envelope for the story's return if rejected.

If the story is accepted, send off another immediately (tailored to fit the magazine's guidelines). Once you have been successful with an editor it is much easier to avoid the slush pile, but to do so you need to keep your name and high quality work in the editor's mind.

Articles:

Send an informative query letter with a strong, original theme. An outline of the proposed article, showing how you are going to treat the subject matter and giving the intended word length, should accompany the covering letter. Mention previous successes and include clips if you have any and state why you would be the right person to write the article.

The wrong approach

Fiction:

Telling the editor that your mum, granny, next-door neighbour, or anyone else, loved your story is only going to get it rejected unread. Saying in the covering letter that other magazines have rejected it, or sending a dog-eared copy that has clearly been out a few times, will also shorten the rejection period.

Stating the story is based on actual events is another no-no. If the story is well written and believable it will sell, regardless of whether it is pure invention or actually happened.

Articles:

Sending the full article implies this was something written on spec and you are hoping it will find a home. Telling the editor how clever, interesting, or funny, the article is will not win you any friends. Your outline should speak for you and convince the editor to commission the piece.

To summarise:

- Research the magazine
- When work is accepted, immediately submit more
- Tailor the query letter so that you appear professional
- Include clips when pitching an idea
- Mention previous successes
- Never say you are a beginner
- Follow the magazine's guidelines

Editors – Who They Are and What They Do

Many small publications are run by one person, who is accountable for all the editorial work, while larger magazines and publishers divide the workload between several different people, all with their own area of expertise. Below are the most commonly used job titles for these editors, and their responsibilities.

Commissioning editor

In magazine publishing, the commissioning editor will assign writers to produce non-fiction articles and features. In book publishing, the commissioning (or acquisitions) editor has a major role in developing the publisher's book list by identifying current trends and spotting gaps in the market. The commissioning editor will be involved with a book and its author every step of the way, from assessing the initial proposal and manuscript, to issuing the author contract and dealing with publication.

Copy editor

A copy editor, whether working on magazines or books, ensures work due for publication is error free. Some copy editors form part of the publishers' staff, and others are employed on a freelance basis. Their role can involve a variety of things, which might include:

- Fact-checking
- Ensuring continuity of presentation
- Checking consistency of style, particularly where co-authorship is involved
- Correcting spelling, grammatical and typographical errors
- Making sure that captions match illustrations
- Checking cross-references
- Querying inconsistency in plot and character traits
- Highlights conflicting statements
- Spotting over-writing
- Flagging up anything potentially libellous

Features editor

Larger magazines often have dedicated editors who are responsible for different kinds of non-fiction content. For example, some of the glossies will have a fashion editor, a beauty editor, travel editor, and so on. More modest-sized publications might have one feature editor with a wider role who is in charge of all lifestyle content. These editors will decide which work will appear in each issue and commission a freelance, use an in-house writer, or write the features themselves.

Fiction editor

The fiction editor is responsible for reading submissions, and for deciding on a magazine's fictional content. It is a good idea to write to a magazine's fiction editor asking for their style guide. These useful guides will outline the kind of stories which are not acceptable. For instance, some publications will not print stories that involve crime or violence, ghosts, horror, religion, or stories with twist endings.

Managing editor

A managing editor is in charge of all editorial decisions regarding a magazine or newspaper. He or she will manage the editorial team, organise the publication schedule, ensure the work is meeting deadlines, and liaise with printers and distributors.

Picture editor

These editors track down suitable images for use in books, magazines, newspapers, television, advertising, and so on. They are responsible for negotiating the fee with the copyright holder, archive, or picture library, for using the image, and for commissioning photographers to provide new ones.

Envelopes and sae

See also: Editors, Publishers, Queries, Rejections, Yours Sincerely

You've worked hard producing your manuscript and now you're ready to submit to your chosen market. Make sure the envelope you choose is big enough to contain your work – folding large wads of paper and cramming them into an undersized envelope will shout 'amateur' to any editor.

In general, work printed on standard A4 size paper should be unfolded and mailed in an appropriate size envelope. But it is acceptable to use an A5 size envelope with up to three A4 sheets folded in half.

Unsolicited manuscripts and saes:

If you send unsolicited stories or articles to a magazine,

you should enclose a stamped addressed envelope (sae) for its return if the commissioning editor decides not to accept it for publication.

The sae should be large enough (A4) to take your manuscript unfolded if you intend to send the same copy to another market – although, if it's only a few pages, it's best to print out a fresh copy for each new submission and enclose a smaller sae.

Including an A5 size envelope will mean your work has to be folded to be returned, but the return postage will be cheaper.

Queries:

It is normal practice to include a stamped addressed envelope when sending out a query letter with an outline for an article. There is no guarantee that the editor in question will use it, but it will greatly increase your chances of a reply. Hearing that your proposal is unsuccessful with one publication is preferable to hanging on indefinitely, and means you are free to query another market.

Self-seal envelopes: The preferred choice of most editorial staff, so use this type whenever possible when enclosing a stamped addressed envelope.

Gusset envelopes: These are useful for sending larger manuscripts through the post.

Board and board-backed envelopes: Come in various sizes and will help protect your photographs during transit.

Royal Mail:

In the UK, the revised charges have meant some changes for writers sending manuscripts through the postal system. The Royal Mail now takes into account envelope size, as well as the weight of its contents.

Letters now fall into three main categories: Letter, Large Letter and Packet.

Letter: Up to A5 size (an A4 sheet of paper folded in half), weighing no more than 100g, the maximum thickness being 5mm.

Large Letter: A little over A4 size, weighing no more than 750g, the maximum thickness being 25mm. This is the category that the majority of manuscripts will fall under.

Packet: Anything longer than 353mm, wider than 250mm, thicker than 25mm or heavier than 750g will come under this category. This will apply to larger works, such as book manuscripts.

Check with the Post Office for current postal charges.

To summarise:

- Use an envelope big enough to contain your work
- Enclose a stamped addressed envelope with unsolicited manuscripts and query letters
- Including a smaller envelope for your manuscript's return is cheaper

F

Feedback

See also: *Edit, Editors, Final Checks, Grammar, Originality, Proofreading, Punctuation, Rejections, Revision and Resubmitting, Writers' Groups, ZZZZ – Sleep on It*

One of the most precious gifts a writer receives is constructive criticism. This can come in various forms, some of which are more valuable than others. To make the best use of feedback, the writer must stand aside from his or her work and imagine it had been written by someone else. This is far from easy to do, but, with practice, even the thinnest-skinned writers can distance their emotions from the comments made about their masterpieces.

Editorial response

Anything a busy editor tells you is worth acting on. Very rarely will editors make a personal note on a rejection slip, so if they do, whether about the content or writing style, take the words to heart and act on them to improve your writing. Make sure the next item you submit doesn't contain the same flaws.

A word of warning: Don't make the error of thinking all you need to do is fix the problems highlighted and resubmit the piece. You should only resubmit after corrections if the editor has asked you to do so.

Editorial services

If you have acted on lots of constructive criticism, but still only receive rejections in the morning post, it might be worthwhile paying for a full professional critique of your writing. There are many literary consultancies, but they are not cheap. Always check to make sure they have satisfied clients who are prepared to speak out on their behalf. A good service will have testimonials available from people they have assisted towards publication. Reputable companies will have no hesitation in telling you about success stories you can verify.

Most reputable writing magazines offer critique services at reasonable fees.

Friends and family

Observations from this group are the hardest to evaluate because our nearest and dearest will try their utmost not to hurt our feelings. It is, therefore, necessary to listen very carefully to what is said, and also to what is left unsaid. Sift out the critical remarks from the praise that will be heaped on you. If a comment runs along the line of "I thought it was great, but could such and such really have happened?" it is worth paying attention. The people who know you are highly unlikely to make negative statements just for the sake of it, so something that causes your reader to question the validity of the piece needs looking at.

To summarise:

- Ask friends and family to give honest criticism, rather than undeserved praise
- Always pay attention to editorial feedback; it is both rare and valuable
- If you are struggling to get work accepted, consider paying for a professional critique

Fees

See also: Invoicing, Keeping Records, Kill Fees, Legal

The amount paid to writers for supplying magazines with stories and articles varies enormously. Much will depend on circulation figures and the type of market the publication caters for.

Most magazines in the UK typically pay between 7p and 25p a word calculated per 1,000 words (so £70-£250 for a 1,000-word article). Publications with a smaller readership may pay less, while the big glossies could offer a higher fee.

Magazines' rates of pay are sometimes displayed on their websites, or found in *Writers' & Artists' Yearbook* and *The Writer's Handbook*. Often a listing will say 'payment negotiable' which means it's open to a little bargaining, but are unlikely to pay a lot more than their first offer.

If you're uncertain how much a publication pays for freelance work, enquire before you submit to it. By sending work to magazines on spec, it's generally assumed that you will accept their usual rate of pay. Bear in mind that some markets pay nothing at all. This is true of many small press magazines and local newspapers.

Be sure that any potential fee will cover the cost of researching and writing the article. Some non-fiction pieces – travel features, for example – could see you out of pocket if the fee offered is less than the expenses incurred.

Payment time can vary, too, some editors paying on acceptance and others paying on publication. You may be asked to submit an invoice for the agreed fee before payment is sent.

Flat fees:

These are the 'one-off' payments offered by some book publishers, particularly in the field of non-fiction. If the sum offered is a fair one it could be a better option than royalties.

A flat fee is normally higher than a royalty advance and can work to a writer's advantage if a book sells fewer copies than the publisher originally anticipated.

The options need to be weighed up carefully; the offer of a flat fee usually means you will be expected to sign an 'all rights' contract and will get no further payment, even if the book becomes a bestseller.

To summarise:

- Fees vary depending on circulation figures and market type
- Enquire if a publication pays before submitting
- Ensure the fee covers the initial outlay of researching and writing the article
- Accepting a flat fee may mean giving up all future rights

Fiction

See also: *Agents, Angles, Children's Picture Books, Dialogue, Hooks, Originality, Point of View, Teen Fiction, Theme*

Fiction writers must first and foremost be storytellers. A really good story can still work, even if the writing is slightly weak, but even brilliant writing will not bring a poor story to life.

Stories need to be believable, which is not to say true to life. Very often things happen in real life that would never be believed in a work of fiction. It is the task of the fiction writer to produce a story that engrosses readers and makes them want to find out what happens next – whether in a short story or a novel.

In order to carry this out, certain guidelines need to be followed. The writer has to consider the events which will take place in the story (plot); the people, animals, creatures or space aliens who will be taking part in those events (characters); where everything happens (settings);

what is said, why it is said and how (dialogue); whose head the reader is in during the telling of the story (point of view); the main idea or meaning behind the story (theme) and last, but possibly the most important of all, the writer's way of telling the story (style).

Characters

The reader needs to be able to identify with and care about the characters. They don't necessarily have to be likeable, but they must seem real.

They should be introduced early in the story, preferably before settings, so that the settings can be introduced from their point of view. In other words, if the opening scene is set in a house, we 'see' the house through the eyes and actions of the character.

Characters should be brought to life by their actions, thoughts and dialogue, so that readers can make up their own minds about the nature of each character. The feelings of characters are usually better shown, rather than told by the narrator. Having said that, there are no hard and fast rules about this and sometimes (depending on the way it is handled) telling the reader about a character's feelings can work.

Dialogue

Dialogue is used to develop character or to advance the story and has to seem real. It should mimic, but not copy, everyday speech. If you have ever listened to a taped a conversation you'd be amazed at how often we repeat ourselves and take far too long to get to the point. In writing fiction, that would slow the story down almost to a stop. Always avoid unnecessary or repetitive dialogue.

A small amount of dialect can be used to establish a character, but can be difficult to read if overused. Pronunciation, diction, grammar and catch-phrases are often used to flesh out characters.

Although dialogue is a wonderful tool to get information across, be careful that your characters aren't telling each other things they should already know. I call it 'as you know, George' dialogue. This can happen when the author wants to tell the reader about a previous event which hasn't appeared in the book or short story. For example: "When we went to China and were picked up by the police, I couldn't find my passport, but fortunately you were able to find it back at the hotel and so brought it to the police station and rescued me, George." George would already know all of this, so the dialogue doesn't ring true.

Another point to be careful about is characters repeating in dialogue something the reader already knows. If you have to let another character in on past events, this is the perfect time to tell and not show.

Plot

The plot has to be a plausible and interesting sequence of connected events. Generally the plot can be broken down into a series of intense conflicts, all leading to a climax (the most intense part of the story) and final resolution. Novels often have several layers, using subplots to produce minor climaxes and resolutions.

Point of view

First person point of view tells the story through the narrator's eyes. Everything that happens can only be seen or experienced by the character doing the narration.

Third person point of view means that an author uses one character's POV throughout a scene and the reader can only know the thoughts of that character or see through that character's eyes. When the POV changes, it must be treated as a new scene and this is shown by an additional line of space or three asterisks forming a line-break.

The point of view character's impression of other characters' thoughts and emotions is the only view expressed until a new scene is introduced with a change of point of view. You shouldn't head hop, as jumping from one head to another can be both confusing and alienating to the reader.

Setting

Settings cover the place and period of time where the story takes place. They are used to set the atmosphere and mood, to place obstacles in the way, or to help establish conflict. Their main purpose is to allow the reader to picture the scene and so imagine the world in which the characters are living.

Style

Style is the unique way a writer uses language and finding your own voice is not something that will happen overnight. The more you write, the easier it will be for your own style to form. Write from your heart but revise with your head. Allow your own feelings to shape the way you use words, but don't be afraid to strip out whole passages when you come back to edit. It's called 'killing your darlings' when you remove phrases that particularly please you, but don't really belong in the story you have written.

Theme

The theme of a story is the underlying line running through it. It is imparted to the reader, often without him or her even being aware of it, by events occurring in the story.

To summarise:

- Adding layers to your story gives it depth and interest

- Make your characters believable and well-rounded
- Choose a point of view for each scene and stick with it
- Developing your own unique style takes time

Fillers

See also: *Angles, Anniversary Pitches, Hooks, Markets, and Topics*

Fillers are very short articles, quizzes, handy tips, and snippets of information that magazine editors use to fill in the odd spaces between a publication's main features. They can range from a few words to 500 words and be aimed at all types of magazines.

Many magazines have regular slots for money or time-saving hints, amusing or heart-warming stories, and strange or little-known facts. Another type of filler popular with editors comes in the form of a list: '25 shrubs for small gardens', '10 ways to beat the winter blues', and so on.

It is acceptable to submit several fillers in one go to the same magazine, but be sure that each one is relevant to that particular market.

For fillers between 200 and 500 words, use a separate sheet of A4 paper for each one. Type your name and full contact details in the top right-hand corner, and in the top left-hand corner, the word FILLER. For fillers of 200 words and above, you should include the word count, too.

Leave four or five blank line spaces, then type in your filler's title, use a double line space under that, and write the text beneath.

For fillers which have fewer than 200 words, you can type a few on the same sheet of paper. But don't cram too many in; separate each one with plenty of 'white space' so that each filler is clearly defined. Again, each one should have a title. However, for those consisting of just a sentence or two, there is no need to add the word count.

It isn't necessary to send a covering letter when submitting fillers, but do enclose a stamped addressed envelope for a reply.

To summarise:
- Submit fillers that are relevant to your chosen market
- Use a separate sheet of paper for fillers over 250 words
- Type several shorter fillers on the same page

Final Checks

See also: Accrediting Sources, Biography, Clips, Consistency, Continuity, Covering Letters, Editors, Envelopes and sae, Guidelines, Layout and Formatting, Punctuation, Queries, Title Page, Word Count, Yours Sincerely

Before sealing the envelope, or pressing 'send' on the computer, make sure the work you are submitting has undergone some final checks. A checklist that you keep next to the computer will ensure your submission appears presentable, giving you the best chance of success.

You will find more detailed information on the various topics under each separate heading, but the following aspects should always be checked. Have you
- Addressed the editor by name?
- Made the covering letter as professional as possible?
- Given your address, email and phone number?

- Included a short biography, if requested?
- Edited both the manuscript and letter?
- Included a stamped addressed envelope?
- Not used staples or fancy bindings?
- Listed sources of information for fact-based articles?
- Included clips, if pitching an idea?
- Followed the guidelines?
- Formatted and ensured the correct layout for the market?

Foreign Words and Phrases

See also: *Clichés, Consistency, Dialogue, Feedback, House Style, Jargon and Slang, Markets, Travel Writing*

This is one of the areas that often trips up novice writers, as using foreign words and phrases to add depth to an article frequently has exactly the opposite effect. When writing for travel and country-themed magazines (*Living France*, *Spanish Magazine*, etc.) it is very tempting to show off and use phrases in the language of the target country. Far from impressing the editor with your linguistic skills, you will be showing your lack of experience.

If used sparingly, foreign words can give a flavour of the country being written about, but only use them when it is impossible to achieve the same effect in English. When using foreign words, make sure that the meaning is made clear from the text without the reader needing to resort to a foreign/English dictionary.

Foreign words should be written in italics and have the necessary accents in the correct place. If using Microsoft Word you can access the character map by choosing Symbol from the Insert menu.

Words in common use in English (such as rendezvous,

pronto, macho) should *not* be italicised.

In fiction, if one of your characters is not English, do not be tempted to insert foreign phrases into every aspect of their dialogue. Choose one or two phrases or exclamations and use them sparingly. Often changing the word order gives a better sense of someone exotic, and not comfortable in English, than littering the page with foreign words.

To summarise:

- Overuse of foreign words shows inexperience
- The meaning should be clear from the text, without the need for a dictionary
- Foreign words should be written in italics, all accents being in place
- Do not italicise foreign words in common usage in English

G

Grammar

See also: *Covering Letters, Dialogue Punctuation, Editors, Final Checks, House Style, Jargon and Slang, Proofreading, Punctuation, Rejections, Spelling and Grammar, Yours Sincerely*

If grammar is a weak point, the best advice we can give you is to buy a book of basics and study it thoroughly. Grammar rules can be, and often are, broken, but you need to know the rules before you can get away with breaking them for effect.

Sentence structure and length

- Keep sentences easy to read and don't use long words if a simple one does the trick.

- Avoid, wherever possible, use of the passive voice (the cake was baked by the chef – passive; the chef baked the cake – active). A good test to check for overuse of the passive voice is to set your edit function to search for variants of the verb 'to be'. If your prose is littered with 'was' and 'were', it is fairly certain you are using the passive voice.

- Sentences should be approximately between 15 and 30 words, although the occasional shorter sentence can be used very effectively. However, using short sentences all the time can give a clipped feel to your writing.

- Vary sentence and paragraph lengths for variety, but do adhere to the style favoured by the target publication.

- Each paragraph should follow on logically from the one which preceded it.

Split infinitives

An infinitive is the root form of the verb: to be, to go, to perform, to write. Splitting an infinitive simply means inserting a word between the 'to' and the verb. The most famous example of this is the line from Star Trek: *To boldly go*.

From a grammatical point of view, all split infinitives are incorrect and should be avoided. You may find your target magazine allows the use of them, but it is far better to get into the habit of not splitting infinitives.

Vocabulary

Pitch the level of your vocabulary according to the market. If writing for one of the popular weekly magazines, don't use words that would require the reader to reach for a dictionary. Similarly, when writing for an upmarket political publication, don't use vocabulary that insults the intelligence of your audience.

The only way to ensure the correct vocabulary usage is by conducting proper market research of your target publication.

- Count the words in the sentences
- Note how many words of three syllables or more are used per hundred words
- Count the sentences in the paragraphs
- Is the tone mass-market, mid-market, or highbrow?

Groundwork or Guesswork

See also: *Accrediting Sources, Continuity, Research*

Do the groundwork and check your facts. This is crucial in both fiction and non-fiction writing and should never be passed over.

Submitting copy which contains factual inaccuracies will almost certainly lose you further work from that publication. The editor will assume you have verified your information and not merely guessed at its validity. He won't be too pleased when readers notice your blunders – and they will – and write to him pointing them out, as this will reflect badly on his magazine.

If you are uncertain of a particular fact, don't just guess at it, look it up. Make use of libraries, reference books, museums, local archives and the Internet.

Call on people you know who might help fill in details. Friends, relatives and acquaintances all have their own areas of expertise and specialist knowledge through their professions, hobbies, or localities.

It's important to get facts right, even when writing fiction. While readers are very aware that a story is made up, most would prefer it to be set in the real world, having locations and historical data accurately portrayed – lose credibility here and you will lose your readers.

Using historical detail

When writing fiction, how well have you researched your facts? If you've set a story in 1830, would your hero be using Morse code? Could one of your characters be chewing bubble gum in 1925, or be solving a crossword puzzle in 1900? If you are using this kind of detail in your story, consult a few reference books to avoid historical blunders.

To summarise:

- Ensure your work is factually accurate
- Call on the expertise of people you know
- Double-check historic dates

Guidelines

See also: *Angles, Anniversary Pitches, Fillers, House Style, Markets, Queries*

Whatever market you hope to sell to, always study the writers' guidelines. These are often displayed on a publication's website, or can be obtained by contacting the editorial department.

Every publication has specific requirements that its writers are expected to adhere to; sending a 3,000-word short story, when the magazine only prints those of 1,000 words, or an email attachment when the editor prefers to receive submissions as hard copy, will result in rejection.

Follow the guidelines to the letter. Stay within the specified word count, use the favoured style and tone, and write and send your submission in the magazine's preferred format. Note, too, whether it wants proposals, or the full article.

Many magazines have different 'departments'. These might include things like a travel piece, a humour slot, or a 'real life' story. Each department will have its own required word count and details of each will be included in the guidelines.

Editorial calendar

This calendar is often planned a year ahead. It tells the writer what the editor hopes to cover in the coming months. By studying the editorial calendar, you can see instantly which topics he will be most interested in, and when.

A magazine's main features may be written in-house, or assigned to a regular contributor, but if your article or filler idea is good and you've angled it to fit the planned editorial, your work will be considered.

Not all magazines publish an editorial calendar online. If it isn't, then email the editor asking if one is available.

Lead times

Pay particular attention to a magazine's lead time. This

is the amount of advanced time that short stories and articles must be submitted in order to be ready for publication in any given issue.

Writers' guidelines and editorial calendars will tell you what the publication's lead time is. As a general rule, a weekly magazine will be working three months in advance, and a monthly magazine, four to six months. Seasonal articles (St Valentine's Day, Easter, Halloween, Christmas, and so on) require the longest lead time, and will need to be submitted at least six months ahead of the publication date.

To summarise:

- Send for writers' guidelines and follow them to the letter
- Study the editorial calendar and angle your work to fit
- Note the lead times and submit copy in plenty of time

H

Hooks

See also: *Angles, Anniversary Pitches, Competitions, Feedback, Fiction, Humour, Markets, Originality, Queries, Teen Fiction, X Factor*

Hooks are words that grab readers and make them want to find out what happens next. A hook will ensure an article is read to the end, or a short story is finished. In a book, hooks make readers turn the pages, whether in a non-fiction or fiction work.

Articles

An eye-opening and original introduction to an article, that causes an editor to look twice, is almost guaranteed to be accepted, because she will know that it will have the same effect on her readership. When pitching an idea for a feature, it is a good idea to use the opening few lines of your article as the introduction in your query.

Competitions

A competition judge will have to read several hundred entries, often on the same theme. How do you make your entry stand out from the rest? Open it with an attention-grabbing hook. The first few sentences of a short story are crucial, and often the only chance you have of making a favourable impression.

Fiction for magazines

As in the case of competitions, your work has to stand out against the hundreds of submissions magazine editors receive every week. Ask yourself, and be honest, if you had to read hundreds of short stories, does your story have enough punch in the opening lines to ensure the editor will read on?

Non-fiction

The chapter and sub-headings should be intriguing enough for a reader to want to find out what each section contains.

Novels

In a work of fiction, it is necessary to set up hooks at the beginning and end of each chapter. Open the chapter with a point of conflict, or drama, and end it with a cliff-hanger. The next chapter should start with a hook, but not resolve the cliff-hanger from the preceding chapter until several paragraphs in. This will keep readers turning the pages to find out how the problem is resolved. End the chapter with another cliff-hanger, and so on.

To summarise:

- The opening of your work is very often the only chance you have to impress
- Open and close novel chapters with a hook
- The opening hook of an article gives the opportunity to show originality

House Style

See also: Consistency, Dates, Foreign Words and Phrases, Grammar, Guidelines, Markets, Punctuation, Quotes, Sidebars, Word Count

House style is the term used to cover a magazine's preferred usage. It will determine how you should deal with various aspects and should be followed to the letter when writing your article. If you are unable to find the guidelines for house style, then it is necessary to research at least three copies of a magazine and make notes on the following:

- Addresses, telephone numbers – how are these written?
- Abbreviations – be consistent in usage
- Article, paragraph and sentence length – count the words and write according to the house style
- Capitalisation and treatment of foreign words – this will vary according to the type of magazine
- Dates, time and opening hours – how are they written and/or abbreviated?
- Grammar – is the publication rigid or does it have a more relaxed approach?
- Italics – when, how and why does the magazine use them?
- Measurements and Distances – look at how they are written and abbreviated
- Numbers – does the magazine write numbers up to ten and use digits after 11, or after another number, or not use digits at all?
- Sidebars – exactly what information, and in what format, is given to the reader?

Humour

See also: *Clichés, Dialogue, Legal, Markets, Originality*

Using humour in fiction, or an article, is not as easy as it might appear. For the humour to work, it must seem natural and unforced. Anything contrived, or overdone to show how clever the author is, will be rejected. Remember that there is a major difference between writing a joke and writing a humorous article. In the first, the punch-line is everything, in the second, the story you are telling is the most important aspect.

Humour should be used sparingly to be most effective. Use the 'less is more' approach to inform and, at the same time, amuse your readers. The humour should arise naturally from the series of events in the article.

If attempting to lighten a heavy topic, always make sure the humour is appropriate to both the subject matter and the publication's target readership. This is particularly necessary with satire. A light touch, as well as a careful eye for libel, is required when penning satirical articles. Only use double entendres and sexual wit if it is clear the magazine accepts that type of humour.

To summarise:

- Never force the humour, or contrive the situation
- The story is the most important aspect
- Use humour sparingly for the best effect
- Only use humour that is appropriate to subject matter and readership
- Satirical articles need careful editing to avoid legal problems
- Sexual wit should be considered only if the magazine has a history of using that type of material

I

Illustrations

See also: Children's Picture Books, E-books, Guidelines, Photography, Public Lending Right

Artwork for children's books

It is not necessary to supply illustrations with the text of a picture book. Illustrators are chosen by the publisher; their style will be carefully matched to best suit a particular story. If you are an illustrator, contact the publisher's design department with examples of your work. Approaching a children's book publisher with a complete package of words and pictures may result in rejection if the publisher likes the illustrations, but not the text, or vice versa.

Artwork for greetings cards

Because text is often bought without illustrations, if you are a writer and an illustrator, it is worth contacting card publishers to establish whether they accept approaches from freelance artists, and to ask what their individual requirements are – some are happy to see sketches, while others prefer to see completed designs. Send examples of your work in the first instance as photocopies, laser copies, or photographs, but never send originals.

Graphics

These are the visual aids used by some technical publications to help make information clearer to the reader. Use of these will vary for each magazine and it is essential to follow the editorial guidelines to discover whether you are required to supply the graphics, or simply supply the information.

Graphs: A basic graph illustrates how variables relate to each other.

Tables: Tables are used to make comparisons between large quantities of information, having data in columns that can be read horizontally and vertically.

Bar charts: These contain vertical bars that look like skyscrapers, used to show trends and variable information.

Flow charts: Displayed as boxes and directional arrows, and used to show steps in a process.

Pie charts: These are the round pie-shaped charts which show proportions, and illustrate data as 'slices' of the pie.

Photocopies

Certain types of publications, such as general history and family history magazines, use old documents to illustrate their articles. These pictures are normally sourced by the writer and ideas for illustrations should be suggested in your initial proposal.

It is important to seek permission from the holding repository to use the documents in this way, as there may be copyright issues to take into account. This should be done before approaching the editor with your ideas.

Photocopies must be clear and easily read. They are usually mailed, unfolded, but the editor may suggest you scan them and send via email.

Sourcing pictures

The simplistic clipart images used by some magazines will have been sourced in-house. But, as many publications don't have their own picture libraries, or appointed picture researchers, providing the editor with images to accompany your article will help to sell your work.

It isn't always practicable to supply your own illustrations – if you're writing an article about

Rembrandt, or the Tutankhamen treasure, for instance – so source your own images from picture agencies and libraries and provide the editor with the details. This should include the agency's website address and the picture's location and reference number.

Picture libraries charge fees to use their images and these fees are the editor's responsibility; remember, you are simply saving the editor time by supplying the information.

Lists of picture agencies and libraries can be found in *Writers'& Artists' Yearbook* and *The Writer's Handbook*.

To summarise:

- Send examples of your artwork, never the originals
- Supply the type of graphics favoured by your chosen market
- Seek permission from the holding repository to copy documents for publication
- Source pictures to accompany your articles

Inclusive Language

All writers should bear in mind that language is continually evolving and that, over time, meanings, usage and expressions change. Using inclusive language in your work allows you to communicate accurately and effectively with your reader; being aware of, and avoiding, the use of any words which might cause offence to, or exclude, certain groups of people.

The type of language you use will depend, to a large extent, on the audience you are writing for. The main areas of language use where negative attitudes arise are those dealing with age, disability, gender, race, religion and sexuality. It is vital, therefore, to study previously published content before writing for, and submitting to, your chosen market.

What might be considered discriminate use?

- Describing an individual, or a group, in a stereotypical, preconceived, or negative way, such as suggesting that all male football fans are hooligans
- Singling out, or giving unnecessary prominence to, an aspect such as disability or gender
- Using a term to describe a group, or an individual, which has been forced upon them rather than approved by them

Age

Many UK publications prefer to use the term 'older people' rather than 'pensioners' or 'the elderly', while US markets often use the word 'seniors' to describe anyone over a certain age.

- Avoid using a negative approach when writing about older people
- When using examples, include a variety of age groups
- A person's age should be given only where this is relevant

It is unnecessary to give family status where this has no bearing on a particular topic.

Example:

Coventry businesswoman and grandmother of three has won the Queen's Award for … is incorrect

Disability

As in the age example above, you should never define people by their disability.

Avoid the following:

- Negative descriptions such as 'victim' or 'afflicted'
- Patronising words such as 'plucky' or 'courageous'

when what you really mean is the person is a success at what he does

- Assuming everybody who has a similar disability is the same, or has the same needs
- Outdated words such as 'handicapped'
- Terms such as 'wheelchair-bound' or 'confined to a wheelchair'. Instead use 'wheelchair user'

Use inclusive language to identify individuals:

By doing this you are calling attention to the person before his or her disability.

People who have autism – not 'autistics'

People who have a hearing impairment – not 'the deaf'

Gender

At one time, it was usual to use the generic term 'man' or 'he' when referring to every human being. This practice still occurs, there often being an apologetic explanation for its use in a book's foreword. The fact is it can appear clumsy on the page, and tedious for the reader, to encounter numerous instances of 'he or she', or 'he/she', or even 's/he' throughout an entire book, along with countless 'his or hers', or 'him or her'.

It isn't always easy to find suitable alternatives to 'he or she' and 'his or her' and even experts can't agree. Some advocate the use of 'they' and 'their', but strictly speaking mixing a singular with a plural is grammatically incorrect and many publishers will object to it.

Example:

A reader (singular) will buy books by their (plural) favourite authors

Ways in which you can re-write:

If you are referring to both sexes, you can often avoid the pronoun 'he' or 'she' by switching to the plural.

Example:

- Supply each delegate with **his** name badge as soon as **he** arrives
- Supply delegates with **their** name badges as soon as **they** arrive

Remove the pronoun 'his' or 'her' from a sentence.

Example:

- It is imperative that a writer edits **her** work carefully
- It is imperative that a writer edits work carefully

As long as it isn't overused, the double pronoun works well.

Example:

- Every chef has **his** speciality
- Every chef has **his** or **her** speciality

Or, as we have often done in this book, you can vary the use of male and female examples in your work in order to present unbiased, non-stereotypical gender roles.

The popular school of thought is that words, wherever possible, should be made non gender-specific, thus promoting parity between the sexes. The key is to follow a publication's own house style.

Examples:

Doorman – door attendant

Manpower – workforce

Housewife – home maker

Chairman – chair

Sportsmanship – fair play

Forefathers – forebears or ancestors

Manmade – synthetic

Mankind – human race

Fireman – fire fighter

Race and religion

If it is relevant to cite people's race, religion or ethnic

background, use terms such as 'the Jewish community', rather than 'the Jews', or 'the Muslim scholars' rather than 'the Muslims'.

Be aware of causing offence and always use the term favoured by the individual. This might be Black, Asian, Afro-Caribbean, mixed race and so on. Don't use expressions like 'coloured', 'half caste' and 'non-white'.

Sexuality

Avoid using the expression 'homosexual'. Today's preferred terms are gay men, lesbians and bisexuals.

When writing about personal and domestic relationships, it is becoming more common to use the all-inclusive term 'partner', thus avoiding setting apart same-sex and unmarried heterosexual couples.

To summarise:

- The language you use will depend on the audience
- Don't write with stereotypical, preconceived, or negative attitudes
- Never give unnecessary prominence to age, disability, gender, race, religion or sexuality

Indexing

See also: Books, E-books, Publishers – When and How to Approach Them, Research

A non-fiction book usually requires an index. The responsibility for providing this is decided during the preliminary negotiations with the publisher and the decision should form part of the contract.

The purpose of the index is to make it easier for the reader to find particular entries and also to discover related subject matter. Good indexing is a skilled occupation and is best left to the professionals. The Society of Indexers has a register of qualified people, each indexer's speciality being listed (www.indexers.org.uk). The cost depends on the complexity and length of the book to be indexed.

If, for financial or other considerations, you wish to tackle the indexing yourself, the best place to start would be requesting the booklet available from The Society of Authors, *Indexing Your Book* by John Vickers (www.societyofauthors.org). This booklet sets out in simple terms the concept and practicalities of the job, recommendations for further reading are listed at the end.

Indexing is normally carried out at page proof stage and sufficient time should be allowed for this.

Useful definitions

Entry: this consists of a heading and one or more page references

Heading: the word or words representing the term, phrase or concept in the book

Subheading: used to divide headings into smaller sections where needed for clarity

Cross-reference: a method of linking related headings and subheadings

To summarise:

- Most non-fiction books require an index for the readers' ease of reference
- Indexing is a specialised skill
- It is possible for a non-skilled person to index a book, but the result is likely to be inferior to that done by a professional

Interviews

See also: Angles, Markets, Research

Magazine editors are always keen to run stories on celebrities, people in the news, and personal profiles of interesting people relevant to their readership. Offer her an interview with such a person and your submission will almost certainly be considered.

It needn't be an interview with a top Hollywood star for one of the major gossip magazines, but it must be targeted at a specific market – a successful woman interviewed for a business journal; someone who has an unusual collection for an antiques and collectables magazine; a local sports personality for a county publication, and so on.

If it's a well known personality – either locally or internationally – your prospective editor won't be interested in publishing the stuff her readers will already know, so aim to provide something new.

1.   Do your homework to discover all you can about the person.

2.   Angle the interview having your target publication firmly in mind.

3.   Write down the questions you want to ask before the interview.

4.   Try to get a different perspective – avoid the obvious questions.

5.   Phrase questions to elicit more than a 'yes' or 'no' answer.

Interviews can take place by email, over the telephone, or in person. Using a tape recorder is a good idea, but ask first if the interviewee is comfortable with this.

Sometimes the person you have interviewed will want to approve your copy before it is submitted for publication, but you should avoid agreeing to this, if possible. If you were granted an interview on the understanding that the piece was to be approved first, you should make it understood that you are prepared to amend factual inaccuracies only.

The way in which you write up your interview will depend on the preferences of your target market. Some magazines publish interviews in a straight 'question and answer' format, while others prefer them written as feature articles, so study back issues of the magazine and follow the writers' guidelines.

To summarise:
- Angle the interview to suit a specific market
- Avoid agreeing to the interviewee approving your copy
- Write up the interview in the publication's preferred format

Invoicing
See also: Fees, Keeping Records

Many, but not all, magazines will ask you to send an invoice for payment; this requirement is usually mentioned at the acceptance stage, along with the fee offered.

Invoices can take any number of forms, but should include all the relevant information:
1. The magazine's title and address
2. The editor's name
3. Your name, address, email and phone number
4. The date the invoice is sent
5. Details of service provided
6. A reference number
7. The amount due

Set up and save a basic template in 'Table' if you are using a computer; adjust to fit A4 size paper. Print out and mail, or email, as per the editor's instructions. Amend the reference number for each consecutive sale, and keep a copy of all invoices you send for your own records.

Title of magazine Address of magazine	Your Name Address Phone number Email
Editor's name	Date
Invoice for article: 'How I Made My First Million'	
Reference number: 0001	Amount due: £100 Thank you

To summarise:
- Include all the relevant details
- Set up a basic template
- Keep a copy of your invoices

J

Jargon and Slang
See also: Articles, Guidelines, House Style, Markets

Depending on the market, some jargon and slang may be permissible, or even, in the case of jargon, required. To decide on the level to which either may be used, it is necessary to carefully research previous copies of the publication.

Jargon:

If writing for a readership knowledgeable on a topic, such as a specialist, technical, or trade magazine, it would be acceptable to use words, phrases and acronyms common to the subject. However, if the same basic article is aimed at a general interest market, all such jargon should be avoided. Using technical or 'insider' terms doesn't make the author appear clever, it simply alienates the reader. For example, it is unlikely that anyone outside of the writing world would understand the term 'opening hook'.

Slang:

When writing an article, the use of slang is determined by the magazine's readership. Some magazines, such as those aimed at a younger audience, use lots of 'in' words and phrases, others will not tolerate any slang. The only way to determine whether or not to use slang in a feature is by studying the market.

In fiction, the use of slang can be very effective in creating believable and easily recognisable characters, but be careful, as slang dates very quickly. What is cutting edge and quirky this month, could be old-fashioned and dated by next. If you decide to use slang terms in dialogue, try to avoid using anything that you think will have a short shelf life. For example, the current slang usage of 'owned' means to make a fool of or embarrass someone or to prove them wrong, but what will it mean in a year or two's time?

To summarise:

- Jargon should only be used when the audience is knowledgeable on the subject
- Use of slang is dependent on the market
- Slang dates very quickly, so should be used with caution

K

Keeping Copies

See also: *Markets, Publishers, Rejections, Revision and Resubmitting*

Whether it's a short story, an article, novel, or competition entry, never submit the only copy you have of your manuscript. Saving work to your computer's hard drive is fine, until something drastic happens to the machine and you find you've lost everything. Play safe and keep a back-up copy of all your work, either as a paper printout or on a disc.

Manuscripts can get lost in the post, either on their way to the publisher, or en route from the publisher to the printer, and things have been known to go astray in busy editorial offices.

Your precious manuscript, sent to an editor on spec, may never be returned to you, or might be sent back dog-eared or coffee-stained. It could even be damaged in transit. Should your manuscript look the worse for wear, always print off a fresh copy before resubmitting to another market – no editor will want to consider work that has obviously been rejected by a rival publisher.

To summarise:
- Never submit your only copy
- Print off your work, or save to discs
- Replace damaged copies before resubmitting

Keeping Records

See also: *Invoicing, Multiple Submissions, Public Lending Right, Revision and Resubmitting*

Getting ahead in the writing world means you not only

have to be creative, you must be businesslike, too. You need to devise a system which will show you, at a glance, the state of play of all your submissions – what has been sent where, and when.

By organising your work in this way, you'll know precisely how long an editor has held on to your work, whether it's time to send him a reminder, or resubmit a rejected piece elsewhere.

Whether you create a spreadsheet on your word processor, or draw columns in a notebook, your headings should include the following:

- Title of work
- Where submitted
- Date sent
- Accepted or Rejected
- Fee due
- Date invoice sent
- When paid

Financial records:

You will also need to keep records of earnings for the Inland Revenue. Note down your income and outgoings, and hold on to relevant receipts.

In the UK, a tax system called Self Assessment came into force in the tax year 1996/97, which means the onus is now on the individual to declare his or her income and expenses correctly.

Taxable income includes: fees, advances on book sales, royalties, reimbursed expenses, and so on, whether the income is from a UK or an overseas source.

There are various allowable expenses which can be deducted from your writing income. These include things like: computers and software, Internet, telephone calls, travel, postage, stationery, printing costs, reference books, etc.

The above list of deductible expenses is by no means exhaustive. As the laws governing tax are subject to change, we strongly recommend that you contact your local tax office for full, up-to-date details.

To summarise:
- Draw up a submissions spreadsheet
- Note income and expenses for tax purposes
- Contact your local tax office for up-to-date information

Kill Fees

See also: Editors, Fees, Guidelines, Invoicing, Keeping Copies, Keeping Records, Markets, Professionalism, Queries, Rejections, Revision and Resubmitting, Serial Rights

A kill fee is a percentage (usually fifty per cent) of the original fee agreed with an editor for a particular piece of work, which is then subsequently not published.

When a piece of work has been accepted by an editor, whether submitted on spec or commissioned, the author is entitled to payment at the magazine's usual rate, or that agreed at time of acceptance. If the editor decides not to use the article at a later stage, the author can submit an invoice for a kill fee.

Similarly, if an editor commissions an article, but rejects the finished piece, the author can claim a kill fee. The exception here is if the final work submitted is so poorly presented that the editor is unable to use it.

Not all magazines pay kill fees. If you submit work to a publication whose guidelines state that kill fees are not paid, you have effectively accepted their conditions, and cannot claim a kill fee if commissioned work is not used.

Acceptance of a kill fee does not affect your rights and you would be entitled to resell that piece of work to a rival publication.

To summarise:
- A kill fee is a percentage of the original fee
- It is only payable if an accepted piece of work is not used
- If guidelines state no kill fees, sending work is an acceptance of this clause
- A kill fee does not affect your serial rights in the piece

L

Layout and Formatting

See also: Books, Computers, Fiction, Final Checks, Guidelines, House Style, Keeping Copies, Publishers, Teen Fiction, Title Page, Yours Sincerely

Bullet points

Bullet points are useful devices when you want to draw your reader's attention to specific information. Readers find them pleasing to the eye because they break up blocks of text, making relevant information easier to find.

Some writers use numbers (1, 2, 3) or letters (a, b, c) when bullet points would be more appropriate. Writing lists as 1, 2, 3, might indicate an order of importance, so use these only if that is your intention: for example, use them in a step by step guide where each point needs to be specified chronologically.

Use bullet points, in place of numbers or letters, when the information on your list doesn't need to be in any particular sequence, or is of equal importance.

A bullet point is used as a brief summary to illustrate a key point in an article. Decide what your key points are and use a separate bullet point for each one.

It doesn't matter whether your bullet points start with a verb or a noun, or whether you use complete sentences, but each bullet point list should have a consistent structure. A list beginning with a verb makes your work appear more active, while a noun gives it a more formal feel.

For example:

Verb

- Use bullet points to enhance your writing

- Indicate a chronological sequence by using numbers
- Select the best structure to suit your list

Noun
- Bullet points can be used to enhance your writing
- Numbers are best used to indicate a chronological sequence
- Structures differ, so choose one that best suits your list

Unless you have used a complete sentence, there is usually no full stop at the end of a bullet point.

Look at the way in which your target magazine uses bullet points and match their usual format; these small details can often make a difference between an acceptance and a rejection.

To summarise:
- Indicate priority by using numbers or letters
- Use a consistent technique
- Match the style of your target market

Chapter formatting for books

When submitting a book to a publisher, a table of contents is often required. It is possible to do this manually, but looks more professional, as well as being easier to manage and update, if it is done using the function in Microsoft Word.

Single headings:

Step one

If the book is already complete, you should start by reformatting all the chapter headings. Highlight the heading for chapter one, click on the drop-down menu, found to the left of the font menu, and choose 'Heading 1'. Go to the heading for chapter two and repeat the process until all chapter headings have been formatted.

If you are just starting out, and have not yet written your

book, simply type Chapter One, or whatever you want as a chapter heading, and format it as described above.

Step two

When all the chapter headings have been formatted, go to the very beginning of your document and place the cursor to the left of the first word on the page. From the Insert menu, choose Break, then Next page and click OK. You should now have a new page at the start of your document.

Step three

Leave the cursor at the top of the new page and click on Insert – Reference – Index and Tables. A new window will open, click on the Table of Contents tab.

Step four

Click on Modify (to the right of Options) and a new window (Style) opens, which enables you to choose the font type and size that will appear on your chapter listing page.

The Style menu contains a list of TOC numbers (Table of Contents). Make sure TOC 1 is highlighted and click Modify.

From the new window (Modify Style) choose the font type, size and style you wish to use on your table of contents page. Make sure 'Automatically update' is ticked and then click OK in all of the windows until you return to your document.

You will now have a chapter list which has hyperlinked pages, which means you can go directly to any chapter from the list by clicking on it.

If you wish to add new chapters, simply make sure that the new chapter headings are formatted as 'Heading 1' following the instructions in step one.

Step five

Before closing your file you will need to update your

table of contents to incorporate any changes, or additions, to your document. To do this, go to the chapter list at the beginning of your document and right-click anywhere on the table of contents.

On the menu which appears, left-click 'Update field'. Then click 'Update entire field' and click OK.

You cannot enter a table of contents unless there is already something formatted for the table to find, but, from the moment you have typed the words Chapter One (or whatever your first chapter is called) and formatted it, you can start using the above system.

Multiple headings:

For non-fiction books it is often necessary to have sub-headings. To incorporate these into the table of contents, highlight the sub-heading in your document and choose 'Heading 2'. Change font and style as per Step Four, but this time do it for TOC 2.

Returning to the index:

To return to the chapter list from anywhere in your document, press [Ctrl] + Home.

To summarise:

- You cannot insert a table of contents before formatting your headings
- Ensure you have chosen 'Heading 1' from the Style dropdown menu
- For sub-headings, use 'Heading 2'
- Always update the table of contents before saving your file

Fonts

Most editors, agents and publishers ask for submissions in an easy to read font. They are not impressed by fancy fonts or strange colours. Using them may make your submission stand out, but not in the way you hope.

Use 12 point Times New Roman, Arial, or Courier, as

these are generally considered acceptable.

Footnotes and endnotes

See also: *Accrediting Sources*

Footnotes and Endnotes are often used to credit the source of information referred to in a non-fiction book. Any material used by an author which has been written by someone else should be properly cited. See the section on Accrediting Sources for details of how to lay out the references in both text and the bibliography at the end of a book.

In a Footnote (where the reference appears at the foot of the page) it is usual to put only the author's last name, the title of the material and the page number. A full reference to the work should then be made in the bibliography at the end of the book.

In an Endnote (where the reference appears at the end of the document and forms part of the bibliography) it is necessary to put in a full reference to the work cited.

To insert Footnotes or Endnotes using Microsoft Word first make sure you are in 'print layout view' and then click where you wish to insert the mark. This should be following the full stop which closes the final sentence of the reference.

Click on Insert from the menu, then Reference and Footnote. A new window will open giving the option to choose Footnotes or Endnotes. You can change all default settings in this window after you have selected Footnotes or Endnotes.

Next choose the number style you wish to use and whether you want continuous numbering (so that the number sequence runs from the beginning to the end of the book), sectional (each new chapter starts from number one) or, in the case of Footnotes, restarting from number one on each new page.

Regardless of which system you choose, Word will automatically update the numbers each time you add a new reference.

If you remove a reference, move one to a different part of the document, or add a new one midway through, Word will automatically reconfigure the numbers for you.

Headers and footers

Submissions should have your name and the title (or part of it, if it is a long one) in the upper right-hand corner of each page. More follows, mf, or MF should appear in the lower right-hand corner of every page, except the last.

The easiest way to do this, so that it looks professional, is to use Headers and Footers in a Word document. From the View menu, choose Header and Footer. A narrow window will appear containing a range of buttons. The buttons on the left deal with page numbering and those on the right operate the Headers and Footers.

A dotted area will appear at the top of your page having the word Header above it. Click inside the area and choose 'right align' from the standard toolbar menu (alignment buttons are to the right of B *I* U). Type your name, a forward slash, and then the title. Leave a space and then click on the number page button, which is the one next to Insert Auto Text. You will then have something like this – name/title 1.

Run the cursor over the buttons and one will read *Switch Between Header and Footer*, click on this button and the Footer dotted box will open. Choose 'right align' as you did for the Header and then type More Follows, mf, or MF followed by three dots. Click close.

The Header and Footer will now appear on every page. When you reach the end of your document and you wish to remove More Follows … from the final page, you need to insert a break to be able to do this.

Click the cursor to the left of the first word at the top of the final page and then choose Break… from the Insert menu. Choose Next page from the Section break types and then click OK.

Open the Header and Footer from the View menu, click on 'show next' to reach the final page, and then toggle the *Switch Between Header and Footer* button to move down to the Footer. To the left of the Switching button is a *Link to Previous* button. Click on this so that it is no longer operative and then remove the words More Follows … from the Footer. Click close.

Italics

Most computers can produce italics, which are *slanted letters*, but, if you are typing and cannot produce italics, the convention is to underline the words you wish to italicise. The *Oxford Writers' Dictionary* gives detailed guidance on italics, but the following examples are those most commonly used.

Uses:

- For emphasis: The enemy continued firing *after* the ceasefire had been called.
- For contrast: The correct spelling is *in*distinct and not *un*distinct.
- Italics are used to cite titles of *complete* works: such as books, films, magazines, musical compositions, and so on.
  o Shakespeare's *A Midsummer Night's Dream* is a favourite of mine.
  o Martin Scorsese finally won an Oscar for his gritty cop thriller *The Departed.*
- Foreign words and phrases (see separate section in index). If you are not sure which foreign words and phrases should be written in italics, it is best to consult a

good dictionary.

- In biology, genus and species names are italicised:
  o Our member of the genus *Homo* is *H. sapiens*.
  o The chaffinch (*Fringilla coelebs*) is a familiar and attractive garden bird.
- Names in legal cases are italicised: *MacDuff* v *Macbeth*
- Ships names are italicised, but the prefix is not, e.g. HMS *Victory*, SS *Great Britain*

Exceptions:

- Holy books are usually not written in italics. So write: the Bible, the Koran.
- The number of a musical work is not italicised, but the title is: Beethoven's Symphony number 6 – *The Pastoral Symphony*.
- If, for some reason, an entire sentence needs to be stressed, and therefore written in italics, but further emphasis has to be placed on a word or phrase within the sentence, then that part is written in ordinary roman type.
  o For example: *The above rules should* always *be followed.*

Line spacing and paragraphs
General submissions:

Most magazines, agents and publishers will ask for manuscripts to be double spaced. If this is the case, the first paragraph should be blocked to the left (no indent) and subsequent paragraphs indented by half an inch.

Each new chapter, or change of scene, begins blocked to the left, subsequent paragraphs and dialogue being indented.

Email submissions:

If the guidelines state email submissions are accepted,

they will normally say whether to send the document as an attachment, in which case line space and indent as above. If the guidelines ask for work to be submitted in the body of the email, you should use single spacing and leave a line between paragraphs. Do remember that each new section of dialogue should be separated by a line of space.

Margins

For all submissions, other than those sent in the body of an email, you should have generous margins all round. Set your margins for one and a half inches (3.8cm) by going to the File menu and choosing Page Setup. This will open a new window where the margins can be changed.

The reason for the wide margins is a simple one, editors like to make notes and comments on manuscripts and it is easier for them to do so if there is plenty of white space around the document.

Numbering pages

Unless told otherwise, all submissions (other than in the body of an email) should be numbered sequentially, either in the header in the top right-hand corner after your name and the title, or in the footer of each page. To find out how to do this, see the section on Headers and Footers above.

Radio

The way a script is laid out for radio drama is quite unlike that used for short stories. On the cover page, apart from the usual details (see Title Page), you will also need to give an estimate of the amount of time the work will take on air.

Directions for the producer, indicating background effects and locations, are typed in capitals and should be brief, but easy to follow.

Lines of dialogue are numbered from the top of each page and the speaker's name appears in capitals, while the actual speech is in lower case. The BBC prefers the dialogue on each page to start from number one, but other production companies want the numbering to run from beginning to end in an unbroken sequence. Producers will use the page number and dialogue line number to direct the drama. Asking the production company for guidelines is essential.

Make sure you leave a clear space between the name and the words to be spoken.

Example of radio script layout:

NAME OF PLAY by Joe Bloggs

INSTRUCTIONS TO PRODUCER GIVING SETTING AND BACKGROUND EFFECTS.

1. FIRST SPEAKER: Says what has to be said, without using any quotation marks.
2. SECOND SPEAKER: Answers, again without quotation marks.
3. FIRST SPEAKER: (ANGRILY) Says something else.
   DOOR OPENS AND THIRD SPEAKER ARRIVES.
4. SECOND SPEAKER: It's about time you got here.
5. THIRD SPEAKER: The train was late.
   SOUND OF CHAIR SCRAPING AS THIRD SPEAKER SITS DOWN.

To summarise:
- Give an estimate of the length of time the drama will run on the title page
- Number each line of dialogue sequentially
- Instructions to producer, sound effects, and speakers' names are given in capitals

- Dialogue is written in lower case and without using quotation marks

Stage

The layout for a stage script needs to show the act and scene numbers, where the action is taking place, and who is speaking. To make the script easier to read, the second speaker's dialogue is further indented than the first. The third speaker's lines are indented the same as the first speaker.

Basic layout for a stage script:

ACT ONE.   SCENE ONE

> A CONVENT, THE MOTHER SUPERIOR'S OFFICE. THE MOTHER SUPERIOR SITS BEHIND HER DESK, LOOKING DISTRESSED. THERE IS A TIMID TAPPING ON THE DOOR.

MOTHER SUPERIOR   Come in.

> THE DOOR OPENS AND A NOVICE NUN STANDS IN THE OPENING. SHE CURTSEYS AND WAITS.

MOTHER SUPERIOR   Enter, my child, and sit down.

> THE NOVICE SHUFFLES INTO THE ROOM AND SITS ON THE EDGE OF A CHAIR.

> How can I help you?

NOVICE   (Weeping) I have sinned.

MOTHER SUPERIOR We all sin, my child. How have you transgressed?

NOVICE   I'm pregnant.

MOTHER SUPERIOR How can that be? You have not left

100

the convent since you entered two years ago. Who is the father?

NOVICE   I can't tell you. I gave him my word.

MOTHER SUPERIOR Time in the punishment cells will change your mind.

BLACKOUT

ACT ONE. SCENE TWO.

> THE PUNISHMENT CELL.
> THE NOVICE WEEPS.
> MOTHER SUPERIOR
> ARRIVES.

MOTHER SUPERIOR It pains me, but you must be beaten. It is for the good of your immortal soul.

NOVICE   I don't care; I cannot give you his name.

> A NUN STEPS FORWARD,
> CARRYING A SHORT WHIP.

SISTER PORTIA   I'm ready, Mother, shall I begin?

Television

When presenting a script for television, it is important to set it out as clearly as possible. Ensure that your name and contact details appear on everything you submit for consideration. If you have an agent, then you should include his or her details as well.

It isn't necessary to follow a set format, but there are some basic rules which dictate layout.

At the beginning of each scene you need to indicate whether it is to be shot inside (INT) or outside (EXT). Next to this you say where the action takes place and whether it is day or night. Leave a line after this and give

101

details which set the scene (who is doing what and where). At the end of each scene, you type CUT in the right-hand corner.

The following example indicates where capitals and underlining should be used:

TITLE OF MASTERPIECE

1.   EXT. ON BODMIN MOOR. DAY
SARAH IS RUNNING. SHE CONSTANTLY LOOKS BEHIND. IN THE DISTANCE IS A CAR. THE MAN CHASING IS GAINING ON HER. SHE STUMBLES AND FALLS TO THE GROUND.

CUT.

2.   INT. POLICE STATION TWO DAYS LATER. DAY
JOHN ENTERS POLICE STATION TO REPORT HIS WIFE'S DISAPPEARANCE. THE STATION IS BUSY. HE SITS DOWN TO WAIT FOR SOMEONE TO SEE HIM. SERGEANT JONES CALLS HIM TO THE DESK.

JOHN: Blah de blah, blah
SERGEANT JONES: More blah, blah
JOHN: (ANGRILY)   Blah, blah de blah

JOHN BANGS FIST ON DESK. SERGEANT JONES LOOKS SHOCKED. DOOR OPENS AND SARAH STAGGERS IN, COVERED IN BLOOD.

CUT.

This is a very basic layout, but would be acceptable for most production companies. The BBC has more detailed layouts for individual types of production and the following styles can be found online at this page: www.bbc.co.uk/writersroom/scriptsmart

• TV shows (having act breaks)

- Studio-based audience sitcom
- Screenplay – Films and single TV Drama

Legal

See also: *Accrediting Sources, Acquiring Rights, Books, Editors, Groundwork or Guesswork, Illustrations, Keeping Records, Opinion Pieces, Photography, Publishers, Quotes, Research, Serial Rights, Unbiased Opinions*

Contracts

Once a publisher has made an offer to publish your book, you will be required to sign a formal contract. This is likely to be a long and complicated document and you should never sign it without reading it through carefully from start to finish. Below are just a few points on which every author should be clear.

Licence:

The author is granting the publisher a licence to publish a book for a set period of time – often for the full term of copyright. The contract should state clearly when rights granted to the publisher will revert back to the author – when a book becomes out of print, for example.

Advance:

The advance payment is set against the author's future earnings from royalties and the sale of subsidiary rights; in other words, the author will receive no further payment until the publisher has made back the sum paid as an advance. Book advances can vary enormously both in the amount, and in the way they are paid, a new author being offered perhaps between £500 and £3,000. Six figure advances are sometimes paid to first-time authors, but this rarely happens.

The advance might be paid in full on signing the

contract, or half on signing and half when the manuscript is delivered, or a third on signing, a third on delivery and a third on publication.

Royalties:

Most royalties start at ten per cent of the book's retail price; in some cases rates rise to fifteen per cent on higher sales. It is normal practice to receive a royalty statement twice yearly, showing how quickly the advance is being earned and any payment due.

- Alterations: A publisher should not be granted the right to alter work without the author's approval.

- Illustrations: Note who is accountable for providing, and paying for, photographs and other illustrations. The publisher may take sole responsibility for these fees, but, in some cases, payment will be shared between publisher and author.

- Index: In the case of a non-fiction book, if an index is deemed necessary, will this be supplied by the publisher, or will the author need to provide it at his or her own expense?

- Subsidiary rights: These are the 'extras' the publisher might hope to sell by negotiating things such as paperback additions, translation rights, book clubs, audio tapes, radio, television, and so on. Does the contract make specific provision for this and are the fees offered to the author fair?

- Completion date: The contract will specify a date when the completed manuscript should be delivered to the publisher. This should tally with any date discussed when the editor initially offered to publish and should be a feasible length of time to allow for the book's completion.

- Publication date: If possible, try to have this stated in

the contract.

If you have any concerns regarding your contract, you should seek legal advice.

The Society of Authors will vet the contract on your behalf. You can join the society if you have had a full-length work published by a commercial publisher (not a vanity published book) or broadcast, or performed commercially, or if you have had a dozen articles or short stories published. Or, you can join as an Associate member as soon as you have had a full-length work accepted for publishing or broadcasting, but prior to signing the contract.

The Society of Authors
84 Drayton Gardens
London
SW10 9SB
Tel: 020 7373 6642
www.societyofauthors.net

The Writers' Guild of Great Britain is a recognised trade union representing writers in books, poetry, television, radio, theatre, film, and video games. The guild also offers a free contract vetting service for its members.

The Writers' Guild of Great Britain
15 Britannia Street
London
WC1X 9JN
Tel: 020 7833 0777
www.writersguild.org.uk

To summarise:

- Sign a contract only when you've read and understood every clause

- Check who is responsible for providing illustrations and/or an index
- Ensure the contract covers subsidiary rights fairly
- Seek legal advice if you have any concerns about your contract

Copyright

See also: *Accrediting Sources, Acquiring Rights, Illustrations, Keeping Records, Photography, Quotes, Serial Rights*

The laws governing copyright can be extremely complex. The information here is for general guidance and we would suggest you seek advice from someone qualified in copyright law if you are in any doubt about your legal standing regarding a copyright issue.

An author's work is copyright protected as soon as it is written, even if it remains unpublished. In the UK and the European Union, copyright lasts for authors' lifetimes and 70 years following their death. After this time, a written work is usually considered to be in the 'public domain' and free from copyright constraints. There are, however, exceptions to this rule and individual works should be checked before use.

Generally, it is advisable to retain your copyright and not sell it outright to a publication. This means that you are offering to lease your short story or article to the magazine for one-time use (serial rights).

Even if work has been commissioned, a freelance writer retains the copyright unless this has been signed over to the publication in a contract.

Staff writers, on the other hand, have no copyright to the work they produce for their employer during their usual working hours. The employer owns the copyright to the work in this instance.

In a book publishing contract, you are granting a licence

to the publisher, allowing it certain rights in your work in return for specified payments. Most publishers won't ask you to relinquish your copyright and in many ways you would be ill-advised to do so, as this would mean giving up any further claims in your book. These future remunerations might be considerable should the book become a bestseller. You might, however, feel that surrendering your copyright in return for a substantial sum would be to your advantage.

There is no copyright in facts. You must, however, use the particulars in your own words and re-angle the information you find, and the way in which it is written, so that you are creating an original piece of work.

There is no copyright in ideas. Unfortunately, it sometimes happens that several writers hit upon the same idea for a short story or article, this is especially likely if it concerns an anniversary of some kind.

There is no copyright in titles or names. But there is something called 'passing off' whereby you cannot safely use certain words in your title that would suggest you were the author, and therefore the copyright holder, of a well-known title – such as Harry Potter. Similarly, you could be accused of 'passing off' if you used the names of well-known characters from another author's novel or wrote your own novel using a famous author's name.

It isn't necessary to take any specific steps in order to copyright your work, although the use of the recognised copyright symbol © followed by your name and the year will confirm your entitlement to the copyright in a published piece. The symbol can be inserted on the final page prior to submitting your work. It is also a good idea to add these copyright details when displaying your stories, articles, artwork, or photographs on your personal website.

Copyright and co-authors:

Copyright is owned jointly in a book which is written by two or more authors. It is wise to agree some basic rules, and state these in writing, at the start of your writing partnership so that each is clear about where they stand if one, or more, author decides to abandon the project.

Draw up a document outlining the rights held by individuals and what should happen if an author drops out. This can be done informally and doesn't have to be drawn up by a legal professional though it must be signed, and a copy held, by each author. The main points to cover:

- How the workload is to be divided
- How royalties will be split
- Whether the co-writer/s can carry on with the idea if one author pulls out
- If an author leaves, can the remaining co-writer/s use his or her work, or research data?

Copyright and other people's work:

You should never use the work of others without first obtaining authorisation. This can usually be done by contacting the publisher of the book you wish to quote from. If you want to use work which appears on a website, contact the webmaster in the first instance.

Using copyrighted material in this way will almost certainly involve a permission fee and this, depending on the words of your publishing contract, may be your sole responsibility, or a joint one between you and your publisher.

Always get permission in writing from the copyright holder, even if consent has been granted by someone you know in an informal agreement.

You will need permission to use:

- Passages quoted from others' work
- Poetry
- Plays
- Song lyrics
- Musical compositions
- Broadcasts
- Maps
- Photographs
- Artwork
- Computer programs

Moral rights:

An author's moral rights are usually stated in the prelim pages of a book. These rights deal with protecting writers' standing in a copyrighted work and include the right to claim authorship, the right to have the work correctly attributed, and the right to object to the work being used in such a way as to prejudice their reputation. Very occasionally, a contract might ask that authors surrender their moral rights, but it is generally inadvisable to do so for obvious reasons.

For more information on the laws of copyright we suggest a visit to the following website: *www.copyrightservice.co.uk/copyright/.*

To summarise:

- Seek professional advice if you are unsure of a copyright issue
- Retain your copyright whenever possible
- Display your copyright details when publishing work on your personal website
- Draw up a document outlining the rights held by co-authors
- Gain permissions by contacting the publisher of the

book from which you wish to quote

Hearsay

Hearsay is second-hand information – an unverified statement or fact – and something of which non-fiction writers should be particularly wary.

Apart from those that print personal opinion pieces, magazines are only interested in publishing material which is factually accurate. They don't want speculation, assumptions, or rumour, posing as facts. For the editor, misinformation can be costly in terms of the publication's credibility and, if your errors make it necessary for her to print a correction or a retraction, it's unlikely she'll use your work again.

Gather your information from primary sources and never present people's opinions as being fact. Using the claims of others in your articles is fine, as long as it's clear that you are attributing the claim to the person, or organisation, making the statement.

For example:

'Only 30% of people take sugar in their tea' – unverified claim

'Only 30% of people take sugar in their tea, says the UK Tea Council' – attributed claim.

To summarise:

* Avoid using unverified statements
* Never present personal opinion as being factually accurate
* Always attribute claims to those making the statement

Libel

Libel is defamatory writing containing a malicious statement which brings any person into ridicule, contempt, or disrepute.

Fiction:

An important point to remember, when writing fiction, is that a libel action can be brought against you if someone recognises himself from your writing and isn't happy about what he reads. Although the onus in these circumstances will be on him to prove he has suffered ridicule, contempt, or disrepute as a result of what you've written, it is much better to avoid the situation in the first place by:

- Never using real people as characters in your stories
- Never giving your characters the names of people you know
- Never describing personal characteristics or traits of those you know

Non-fiction:

If people believe their reputations may be harmed by something you have written about them, an action for libel can be brought against you. But the person concerned does not have to prove that his or her reputation has been harmed if, in the eyes of the law, something you have written is deemed libellous.

Some important points to bear in mind:

- It is still libellous if a defamatory statement is written as a joke
- An action can be brought, even if a libellous statement was unintentional
- You can be prosecuted for libel if people recognise themselves from your words – you needn't have referred to them by name
- It is not possible to libel dead people, but you should be careful not to make defamatory statements which might be considered to reflect on their living relatives

Legal defences against libel:
There are three main legal defences against an action of libel: 'Justification' which means what you have written is known to be true: 'Fair comment' relates to an opinion based on truth and made in good faith and without malice: 'Privilege' is information gathered by the press to enable them to report accurately on judicial proceedings, parliamentary sessions and public meetings.

To summarise:
- Don't use people you know as characters in your stories
- Comments can be libellous, even if made unintentionally
- People identifying themselves can sue for libel even if not actually named

Letterheads
See also: Agents, Covering Letters, Editors, Publishers, Queries, Yours Sincerely

When you submit a letter to an editor, or agent, you want to impress from the second the page is taken from the envelope. One way of giving your submission a more professional look is by using headed notepaper.

This needn't be an expensive option. In fact, if you have a publishing package on your computer, or you know someone who has, it is possible to design a stylish letterhead. However, do make sure you have a good quality printer and a suitable weight of paper – for this purpose 90gm should be the minimum.

If you do not have access to a publishing package, it is worth the expense of having some letterheads professionally printed.

Keep the embellishments as low-key as possible. The idea is to give a professional appearance, while making sure such items as your street address, email, website (if you have one) and telephone numbers are easy to read.

To summarise:
- Printed letterheads look professional
- All your contact information is available on one page
- Use a suitably heavy paper
- Keep embellishments to a minimum

M

Markets

See also: *Anniversary Pitches, Articles, Editors, Fillers, Final Checks, Guidelines, House Style, Outlines, Queries, Research*

Home

Every week, hundreds of short stories and articles are rejected because their style, length, or subject matter doesn't fit what the magazine publishes. The biggest mistake new and unpublished writers make is to send work out without first studying the market; it's like guessing at the shape of a missing jigsaw piece. And, if you are merely guessing at what the editor publishes, your work won't interest him, no matter how well your manuscript is presented.

Analyse your market:

The key is to write up your ideas into something that is tailor-made to fit your chosen market. The editor should feel that your submission is 'ready to go'; fitting in seamlessly with the magazine's style and other content.

Don't rely solely on the information given in reference books like the *Writers' & Artists' Yearbook*; this can only ever be a general guide. Read several recent copies of a magazine and carefully analyse the content.

1.   How long are the articles and short stories? This is the length you have to write, not more,   not less.

2.   Do they prefer a certain type of short story – gritty, thought-provoking, humorous, or those   having a twist ending?

3.   What sort of articles do they use – true life, self improvement, investigative, nostalgic?

4.   Who is the magazine aimed at? Study what's already

been printed; note the average age of the people in the stories – readers like to identify with the main character. Advertisements are a good indicator of the readers' general interests – do the ads feature young mothers and babies, or retired couples; are they slanted towards new technology, antiques and collectables, or foreign holidays?

5. In what style are the articles written – do they address the reader in a modern chatty way, or are they more intellectual and formal? Does the editor like to use sidebars and include lots of 'useful information' lists?

Magazine markets:

National: The top magazines which everybody recognises from the newsagents' shelves are the hardest markets to break into. Some of these pay better than others, but one thing is certain, all will be inundated with submissions from hopeful contributors. A lot of the content is written in-house, the columns that appear in each issue being written by regular columnists. However, most top publications do accept work from freelance writers, so if you have an idea that you think would suit them, don't be afraid to query the editor.

Local: Almost all counties have magazines featuring stories about the people and places of their locale. The content of these county publications varies widely, but generally they run things like interviews with local people, small business profiles, historic events or heroes, local legends and folklore, wildlife and nightlife.

Trade: This area is often ignored by writers, but just about every trade, profession, or business, publishes a trade, or in-house magazine. Some only accept articles from people who work within the profession, but there are literally hundreds of others, eager to fill their pages with interesting and well-written copy. There are listings for trade and business magazines in *Benn's Media Directory* and most reference libraries will hold a copy.

Specialist: The content of these magazines is devoted to a particular subject. There are hundreds of specialist publications covering all kinds of hobbies and interests from angling to teddy bears and genealogy to motorbikes. Writers for this market need to be conversant with the subject matter, as the readership is likely to be well-informed, but it's a good one to try if you have some specialist knowledge.

Overseas

The *Writers' & Artists' Yearbook* lists some publications in Australia, Canada, New Zealand, South Africa and the USA and *Benn's Media Directory* gives many more. But the most comprehensive guide to American markets is *The Writer's Market*, which is available in both book form and online subscription www.writersmarket.com).

The USA is the main secondary market for UK writers, and the most effective way to gauge suitability is by visiting a magazine's website. Read the online content and any archived articles and stories to judge whether this is the right market for your work, and take note of the editorial guidelines.

When writing for overseas publications, be aware that the spelling of many commonly-used English words vary, so set your computer's spellchecker to your chosen language.

To summarise:

- Study your market before you write
- Match your submission to a publication's usual content
- Make use of your local and professional knowledge

- Expand your sales potential by looking into overseas markets

Marketing

See also: *Press Release, Websites and Blogs*

Seeing your book in print is a thrill for any author, but getting it published is only the beginning. As soon as your book is in print – and often before it has reached that final stage of the publication process – it will need to be promoted.

How well your book is marketed will depend largely on your publisher's marketing budget. Its sales and marketing teams will have ensured your book is featured on the publisher's website, listed in publishing catalogues, and stocked in bookstores.

Prior to the publication of a non-fiction book, you will have been asked to present a list of marketing ideas – ways in which you and the publisher's team will be able to promote the book. In fact, because publicity is vital, producing good ideas and being willing to help with promotion might mean the difference between your book being accepted or rejected in the first place.

Useful ideas

- List local newspapers and county magazines who might run a story about you
- Produce a list of magazines which cover your book's subject, so that relevant critics can be asked to review the book
- Write articles on the same topic for local, national, or online publications and mention your book's title in the author bio
- Offer to give a talk, demonstration, or workshop to a relevant group or society

- Suggest, and be willing to judge, competitions where your book is the prize

Self-published books

You will need to work even harder to market your book if you have chosen the self-publishing route. Without a publisher's team behind you, to assist with promotion, you will need to think imaginatively – every book you sell will be down to your own marketing skills.

As well as using the suggestions above, here are 12 ways in which you can market your self-published book:

1. Give review copies to the local press
2. If you've set your novel in a place other than where you live, send copies to the press in that area, too
3. Offer the book to local booksellers on a sale or return basis
4. Ask the bookstore if you can do a book signing
5. Create a website or blog around yourself and your book
6. Make a sample chapter available on your website
7. Add a short book blurb to your email 'signature'
8. Free handouts – using desktop publishing, design and print off bookmarks featuring your book
9. Get listed on your town or village's website
10. Approach local radio to be interviewed
11. Sell signed copies at local fêtes and fairs; a percentage of your sales going to the cause
12. For a children's book, offer to donate a portion of your sales to school funds – schools are always keen to raise money and to encourage reading

To summarise:

- Come up with ideas above and beyond what your publisher proposes
- Be willing to comply with promotional suggestions

- Think imaginatively to market your self-published book

Multiple Submissions

See also: Angles, Books, Markets, Publishers, Serial Rights

A multiple submission simply means sending the same piece of work to more than one publication at the same time. The rules vary regarding this practice, depending on the type of manuscript involved.

Books

Publishers would prefer to think they were being offered an exclusive manuscript, however, because of the length of time it takes to read and reply to individual authors – often many months – most accept the fact that authors are quite likely to send out multiple submissions.

If you do decide to send your manuscript to more than one publisher, it is important that you make it clear in your covering letter that you've done so. This is not only good manners, but may mean a faster response. If the publisher thinks another house will see the book's potential, he might want to get an offer in first!

Non-fiction articles

The same rules apply as for short stories; don't send the same article simultaneously to two markets. This applies even if you feel the magazines are not rival publications – a specialist hobby, and a general interest one, for example.

You could, of course, use your knowledge and research to write more than one article on the same topic.

As long as each article is sufficiently different, and slanted to fit the remit of your chosen markets, there is no reason why you couldn't offer them to non-competing magazines at the same time.

Short stories

Never send the same short story to more than one market at the same time. Editors want to print stories that are exclusive to their publication and, should they spot the same story in a rival magazine, you'll be added to their blacklist and won't be able to sell work to them in future.

You could, however, send the same story to an overseas market at the same time as submitting it to a UK publication, as you would be offering them different rights – First Australian Serial Rights, First Republic of Ireland Serial Rights, and so on.

To summarise:

- Submit short stories and non-fiction articles to one market at a time
- Offer the same work to overseas markets
- Make it clear to book publishers if your manuscript is a multiple submission

N

Newspapers

See also: *Accrediting Sources, Angles, Groundwork or Guesswork, Jargon and Slang, Layout and Formatting, Legal, Quotes, Research*

For the beginner writer, local newspapers are some of the best places to start. Very often they are actively looking for local news stories to fill their pages. Pieces submitted to a newspaper are called copy and copy relating to a news item is a story. So, when submitting to a paper, don't talk of articles or manuscripts, but discuss copy and the story.

The copy should be typed using double line-spacing and, as for all other typed submissions, wide margins. In the top left-hand corner of the page type your contact details – name, address, telephone and email, under this information put the date.

Again, as for other submissions, use the header to insert the title and page numbering and the footer to put more follows. Although you give a title to your work, you do not supply headlines; this is done by a specialist on the staff.

Newspaper pieces must be brief and to the point; don't fill the page with unnecessary waffle. Keep to the facts and make sure everything is explained and clearly understood. The point of newspaper copy is to inform the reader. Sometimes you may come in on a story that has already been running for a couple of days. You must never assume that every reader has been following the story and will be in possession of all the facts. For every story, the opening lines must tell the reader what the piece is about – this is also true for an on-going account.

Open by stating existing facts and give new information in as few words as possible, but ensure you include the main points.

For example:

'The fire in Watsonia's Warehouse, which so far has claimed four lives, was no nearer to being brought under control this morning. The area cordoned off has now been extended to include North Ward Street and Cornerstone Mews.'

From this beginning you develop the story, bringing in all the facts. End the piece by tying up any loose ends. For newspaper copy, all the interesting bits should be as close to the beginning as possible.

Accuracy in reporting is vital. Only report the facts which you can prove. Anything else, as in things people say they heard or were told, is hearsay until you find the source and can quote from it. Keep your story balanced and give every side's point of view, regardless of your own personal take on a story.

Attribute quotes and give everyone involved the opportunity to refute or agree with the words of others quoted. Double-check dates, ages, addresses and the spelling of names.

To summarise:

- Newspaper articles are called copy
- A news item is called a story
- Open with the facts and give the main points of the story
- Don't waffle
- Accuracy is vital
- Double-check dates, ages, addresses and the spelling of names
- Attribute all quotes and do not use hearsay as facts

- Keep the story balanced, allowing all sides the opportunity to give their view

Nom de Plume

See also: Covering Letters, Editors, Invoicing, Legal, Title Page

It's extremely satisfying to have work accepted for publication and, for most writers, there's no greater buzz than to see their name in a magazine byline, or on the front of a book jacket. However, some writers, for a variety of reasons, use a nom de plume – or pen name – and it's worth weighing up some of the snags against the advantages.

First, why use a name other than your own? Privacy might be an important issue for you, or you might feel it politic to use a nom de plume if writing similar articles, or articles having opposing views, for two rival markets. Maybe you feel you would sell more books if you had a more memorable name. Writers of certain genres often choose names that they believe are more in keeping with their chosen market; a fantasy author called Bert Clutterbuck having less perceived mystique than Raven Gaul.

Some writers choose different names when switching genres and might, for instance, publish children's books and erotica novels, or romantic comedies and political thrillers, under different names.

It is often said that men find it harder to sell short stories to women's magazines when using their own names and so pick a female name when submitting to this market. As a rule, if a story is suitable, it will be accepted for publication no matter what sex the author is, but, if you're in doubt, using an initial and surname is a simpler option than a full-blown gender change.

It would be wise to use a slightly different name if you share one with an already well-known author – this is easily done by shortening a first name or including an initial. If your name really is Jeffrey Archer, you might still be accused of 'passing off' (letting people think you were the famous author), but you could use Jeff T Archer.

But how will using a nom de plume affect how you get paid? When you make submissions to publishers, you should indicate that you write under a pen name and that this is the name you wish to appear as your by-line; your real name should be included in brackets after your pen name on the title page. Include your real name as well as your pen name on all correspondence with the publisher, so that cheques are made out to the name your bank recognises.

Mistakes sometimes happen, and cheques are made out to the wrong name, therefore it's a good idea to notify your bank that you intend to use a pen name, so that it is aware that this might occur.

To summarise:
- Nom de plumes are useful when writing in different genres
- Initials are a simple way of avoiding gender-specific names
- Real and pen names should be included on submissions
- Banks should be made aware that you use a nom de plume

Notebooks

See also: *Angles, Markets, Opinion Pieces*

All writers can testify that story ideas are elusive things; the best ones often rearing their heads at inopportune moments and not necessarily when you're sitting at the computer. This is why most successful writers carry a notebook; recording ideas, snippets of information, snatches of overheard dialogue, and unusual facts that might be developed later into a saleable writing project.

Some like to make lists as a way of brainstorming a subject and this can be particularly helpful when trying to think up new angles for non-fiction articles. For others, a notebook kept near the bed is a handy device to jot down those thoughts that often come just before sleep, or on first waking, but which, if not written down, are soon forgotten.

Some ideas will be utilised, others expanded and fleshed out, and yet more will act as useful prompts. Remember, very few novels, non-fiction articles, or short stories come to a writer fully formed. An idea needs to be developed to its full potential, the resulting writing being honed until it's up to the standard required by an editor, and a notebook is an excellent writer's tool for storing all those seeds of ideas.

To summarise:
- Jot down ideas to develop into saleable projects
- Brainstorm a subject for new angles
- Keep a notebook near your bed

Numbers
See also: *Dates, Final Checks, House Style, Layout and Formatting*

There are certain rules regarding how numbers are dealt with in manuscripts. Wherever possible, it is always advisable to check the house style of the magazine or publishing house you are targeting, as the rules can vary from house to house.

General rules:

- All numbers starting a new sentence or paragraph should be spelt out in full, although it is better, if possible, to rewrite the sentence and so avoid starting with a number
- Always spell out million (five million; 64 million, not 12,000,000)
- Numbers in thousands (1,000; 12,365; 2,500) are usually written with a comma
- Numbers between one and ten should be written. Numbers 11 and above should appear as figures:
- A six-year-old girl, but an 11-year-old boy, but avoid using both in the same sentence. If unavoidable, whichever style is first used should also be used for all numbers in that sentence
- Four years, five days, but 34 years, 23 days
- A seven-metre-square room, but 2,000-metre-square field
- Five miles from Glasgow, but 65 miles from London
- Where a range begins with a number below ten and ends with a higher number, it is usual to write both numbers out in full: between seven and twenty people are expected to attend
- Fractions are usually spelt out: three quarters of a field, a three-quarter view, but in measurements decimals are used: 9.5 kilometres (not 9 1/2 kilometres)
- Per cent is usually spelt out in prose, 11 per cent or six per cent, but % is used for statistics
- For a range of numbers the house style often varies, but it is normal to use the least possible number of

digits (except 10–19), for example: 32–9, 141–75, 100–4, 115–19 and **not** 32–39, 141–175, 100–104, 115–119

Exceptions:

- Distances where the unit of measurement is abbreviated: 5km
- Time of day: 6 p.m.
- Centuries: 9th century
- Temperatures: 7°C

O

Opinion Pieces

See also: Markets, Websites and Blogs

An opinion piece can be on any subject written from a personal perspective. However, the most publishable ones are newsworthy and topical, focussing on current issues and events.

When writing opinion pieces, it's important that your line of reasoning is well formulated, well researched, and doesn't wander off topic, or include more than one central theme. To make any kind of impression, your message should be clear and focussed around your main point.

Be sure that you check your facts; your argument will fail to impress if it contains inaccuracies.

1. Quote people correctly
2. Check statistics before including them
3. Cite any sources you use

Markets:

There are few general interest publications which take opinion piece articles, though most popular magazines have a letters page where readers are encouraged to offer their views on previous content. These publications are unlikely to print letters they consider controversial, or which oppose their ethics or general stance, but welcome those from readers who have found the magazine's subject matter beneficial in some way.

The letters printed in newspapers are usually more 'opinionated' and are often published in order to spark interesting and lively debate amongst their readership.

Professional journals regularly publish opinion pieces and encourage succinct articles from knowledgeable writers who have something to say. Light-hearted and humorous contributions go down well in some journals, while others are looking for subjective content which has a serious message.

Opinion pieces are usually between 500 and 800 words. Staying within the required word count is important when writing for any market, but especially so when submitting an opinion piece. By exceeding the word count, you run the risk of a sub-editor chopping out sentences, so that the piece fits the allocated space. This might mean something you considered to be a vital point is removed from the published piece.

To summarise:
- Keep opinion pieces newsworthy and topical
- Remain focussed on one central theme
- Don't exceed the required word count

Originality

See also: *Angles, Anniversary Pitches, Children's Picture Books, Fiction, Hooks, Queries, Teen Fiction, Theme, Topics, X Factor*

Whether you are writing non-fiction books, articles, short stories, or novels, every editor, agent and publisher is looking for someone who can add a spark of originality to existing themes.

In truth, there are no new themes. Every idea you think of has been done before in one format or another, but coming up with an original and exciting new way to deal with an existing topic, and putting together a well-written and interesting piece, is a sure-fire way to get your work noticed for all the right reasons.

Let's say you are writing an article for Valentine's Day: why not research love in retirement homes?

Hundreds of non-fiction books are written on hobbies, so look for a different slant. Instead of writing only about stamp collecting, why not change tack slightly and include sections on collecting post marks? Include interviews and anecdotes from unlikely and unusual sources. I know someone whose post mark collection is so valuable it is kept in a bank vault, whose reputation is so revered that his collection is shown all over the world. Nothing unusual there for someone wealthy, but this man is a working-class artisan who lives in council housing.

Writing a crime novel? Why not make the sleuth a geriatric cross-dressing former priest?

One of the main reasons otherwise well presented stories are rejected is because the ending is telegraphed from the outset. Be original in how you tackle the plot. If you can keep the editor guessing she will read all the way to end – and most probably accept the story for publication.

To summarise:

- There are no new themes, but there are new ways of dealing with existing ones
- An original approach, and immaculate presentation, gets your work noticed for the right reasons
- Try to think laterally, adding a spark of originality to all your writing

Outlines

See also: *Articles, Covering Letters, Hooks, Originality, Queries, Sidebars, Topics, X Factor, Yours Sincerely*

An outline is needed when pitching an idea to an editor to show the proposed subject matter and how you intend to deal with it. It accompanies your query letter. Before writing an outline, it is essential you know exactly what you are going to write and have done all the research and collating of facts.

Make short notes on each aspect of the article and then juggle them around until you have the feel of the piece. One way of doing this is by writing the ideas on pieces of paper or card and shuffling them into order. You can also type them into a word document, then cut and paste until you are satisfied with the way the article is going to be focussed.

Before you write the outline, start by imagining the editor. She is sitting at her desk opening perhaps the twentieth query letter of the morning and it is only 10 a.m. Out of all the information you have collected for your article, what would make her put your query into the tiny 'maybe' pile instead of the overloaded rejection tray? What is it about the article you intend to write that would capture her interest and make her want to find out more? Whatever it is, that's what goes into the intro section of your outline.

For the layout of the outline, centre your working title a few lines down from the top of the page, your by-line being underneath. Drop down a couple of lines and write your outline.

For example:

Love Me, Love My Article
By
Great Writer

Intro: This is where you put your killer opening: the information being used in such a way that the editor cannot fail to be interested. You could use the first few lines of the article as you intend to write it. Or, you could put in some startling and little-known fact. Or ask a question that demands to be answered.

Main body: This contains the main points of interest and shows the tone the article is going to take.

Ending: Wrap up the ending, so that it ties together all that has gone before into a cohesive whole. It is a good idea to refer back to the intro, if it is feasible to do so.

The outline should not take up more than a page, so keep to the point, but make sure the tone of the article comes through. If you intend to use humour, don't tell the editor that; show her by using humour in your outline.

To summarise:

- An outline accompanies the query letter
- Gather all your facts before attempting to write the outline
- Shuffle the information around until you are happy with the way the article is going to run
- Grab the editor's attention by having a great intro
- Use the same tone in the outline as you intend to use for the actual article
- Make sure the main body covers all the interesting aspects of your proposed piece
- Show how you are going to wrap up the article into a cohesive whole

P

Padding

*See also: Grammar, Revision and Resubmitting, ZZZZ –
Sleep on It*

Some writers turn long-windedness into an art form;
they believe that using five words where they could have
used one will make an impression on an editor. It will,
but not the impression they'd hoped to create, because a
good editor will spot this sort of padding.

Check your writing for clutter. Strike out any redundant
words which add nothing to the sentence's meaning.
Aim to write tightly and avoid repeating information and
waffling.

The company that belonged to Mr Howard can be more
succinctly written as Mr Howard's company.

*The memorable Italian Lakes are unforgettable and will
always be etched on my mind.* This sentence has told us
the same thing three times. The Italian Lakes are
unforgettable would have been enough.

*The market gardener gave me an idea of how long it
would be before the fruit would be ready.* The market
gardener explained when the fruit would be ready.

Expanded phrases increase word count, but add little to
an article's clarity. Concise language is more powerful.

**Some examples of expanded phrases and their tighter
equivalent:**

As a consequence of – because
Be of assistance in – help
At this point in time – now
In the absence of – without
All across the board – all
With the exception of – except

For the purpose of – to

Is in accordance with – agrees

Another way to cut out padding is to avoid empty expressions:

At the end of the day

For what it's worth

When all's said and done

It goes without saying

Wordiness isn't confined to non-fiction. Sometimes short story writers forget that fiction is meant to be like life, but without the boring bits. Short stories are called short for a reason; every scene, paragraph and sentence has to work to move the story through conflict and crisis towards a satisfactory conclusion.

If your story has Jane receiving an important letter, then this is where the story should begin. It isn't necessary to first show her being woken by the alarm, stretching, getting out of bed, having a shower, choosing something to wear, and putting on her make-up before she goes downstairs to pick up the mail.

Padding is what poor writers resort to when they don't have enough story to tell, but need to reach a required word count. Here's how 51 words can be reduced to 6.

Sentence 1: *Mike decided on the spur of the moment that he really didn't want to be in the house with Jane any longer, so quickly took his coat from where he'd left it earlier on the back of the chair and, without even putting it on, opened the door and went out.*

Sentence 2: Mike grabbed his coat and left.

Similarly, when writing a novel, keep focussed on moving the story along. There is more scope in a novel to include descriptive passages, but these should be relevant to the storyline rather than in place of it.

To summarise:

- Cut redundant words
- Write tight – don't repeat information
- Avoid expanded phrases
- Don't use empty expressions
- Keep descriptive passages to a minimum

Photography

See also: *Articles, Illustrations, Markets, Queries*

Very few magazine articles which run to 1,000 words (and sometimes fewer) are published without at least one photograph. At one time, it was down to the in-house picture researcher to source suitable images from press agencies, picture libraries, or museums, but, for most magazines, the days of employing picture researchers are long gone.

Many otherwise interesting and well-written articles are rejected because editorial staff do not have the time to hunt for pictures to accompany them. Therefore, being able to supply the editor with a complete package of text and pictures will greatly increase your chance of acceptance. Not only that, but you'll receive a higher fee for submitting both.

Always tailor your photos to fit the publication, as each will have its own specific requirements and, as in any submission, follow the contributors' guidelines. Study the type of picture the magazine uses – previous issues will show you the style and quality to aim for.

Many editors stipulate that photos must contain people, and by this they mean people doing something. These 'action shots' involve people at work or at play, or interacting with others in some way. For example, to illustrate an article about a chef, you might take a picture of him working in his kitchen, or at a local market in the act of buying fresh ingredients.

Digital

Traditionally, the favoured format for magazine pictures was transparencies (slides), or prints. But now most magazine editors are happy to accept digital images; in fact, some prefer them. The greatest advantage of digital photography is being able to see your pictures at the time they are taken, there being the option to re-take those not up to standard.

You may be asked to burn your images to a CD-ROM and submit by post. Never email digital pictures to the editor unless you have been requested to do so.

Size and quality: A digital picture is made up of many hundreds of pixels, the image resolution being calculated by the number of pixels per inch (PPI). This means that the greater the number of PPI, the better the detail, which ultimately results in a higher quality image.

On the principle that you can always reduce the size of a digital image, but cannot increase its resolution without losing quality, it's wise to set your camera to take pictures at its highest possible resolution.

The pixels also have a bearing on the size of the printed image and your camera's specifications will be the key factor here. Picture quality will be lost if you increase the image size beyond the pixel limitation of your camera.

As an example, taken at maximum resolution, a 2 mega-pixel camera (around 2 million pixels) will produce a high quality picture of 4 inches x 5 inches.

At maximum resolution, a 3 mega-pixel camera (around 3 million pixels) will give you a good quality print of 8 inches x 10 inches. But for a high quality picture of this size you would need a 5 mega-pixel camera (around 5 million pixels).

Labelling

Whatever type of photographs you submit, make sure they are well captioned, but never write directly on the back of your pictures, as ink tends to smudge on photographic paper. Instead, use labels for your contact details and to name your pictures. Include a separate sheet which has relevant details about each photograph and, because photos have a habit of going astray, never send your only copies.

Picture libraries

There are times when it isn't feasible to take your own pictures and you may need to look elsewhere for a suitable illustration. This is when picture libraries can be used. There are dozens of picture libraries, many of which are listed in the *Writers' & Artists' Yearbook* and *The Writer's Handbook*, and most libraries have a web presence.

Thousands of images are available, ranging from the work of one individual covering a specific area, to huge miscellaneous collections. Some libraries are 'rights managed': a fee is shared between the photographer and the library each time an image is used.

Other fees can include service charges, hire, and reproduction fees so, although it's a good idea to source pictures that could accompany your text, thereby saving your editor time, you should not pay for these yourself. Supply the editor with all the relevant details, but let him negotiate the fee with the picture library.

Some libraries offer collections of 'royalty free' images on CD-ROM. These can be obtained for a moderate sum and are useful for writers who can use general images to accompany their work.

Sources for free photos

Another way to supply a 'words and pictures' package is to contact the public relations departments of organisations and businesses. Many of these will gladly provide you with pictures in exchange for editorial exposure.

Some helpful PR departments might include tourist boards, conservation groups, charities, tourist attractions, auctioneers, travel companies, re-enactment groups, animal-aid societies, or sports organisations.

Transparencies

Some editors prefer photos as transparencies. This is particularly true of glossy magazine publishers, who require large, high-quality, detailed pictures. In publishing terms, there are some advantages of transparencies over other formats – the colours are more intense and brighter, and more detail can be obtained in large pictures without resulting in graininess.

To summarise:

- Many articles are rejected for lack of accompanying photos
- Previous issues show the style of picture a magazine uses
- Digital images must be high resolution and excellent quality
- Pictures of people should contain an element of action
- Quality is lost by increasing image size beyond pixel limitation
- Royalty-free images can be bought on CD-ROM
- Photos should be named and labelled with contact details

Plagiarism

See also: *Accrediting Sources, Legal, Quotes*

The Oxford English Dictionary defines plagiarism as '*to take and use the thoughts, writings, inventions etc. of another person as one's own*'.

For writers, plagiarism is the pretence that another author's work is their own, that is, they have deliberately copied something and passed it off as something they had written themselves.

You can be guilty of plagiarism by inadvertently 'lifting' someone else's words. This can happen when writing non-fiction if your research has been limited to one source, because then you will be using only one person's interpretations and opinions of the facts. Always consult several sources, whether original documents, print sources, or from the Web, so that you can form your own ideas and judgements.

When writing fiction, plagiarism can be harder to define. Obviously a story which has exactly the same plot, characters, or dialogue will be open to accusations of copying. This may also be the case if you use an already existing storyline, but hope to disguise it by making a few minor adjustments!

For example:

Original storyline – An artist is murdered on an airplane. Several people on board wanted her dead. The flight attendant, and his partner, the pilot, turn amateur sleuths. During the five-hour flight, and after much clever detective work, they deduce that the murderer is the co-pilot, who hijacks the plane threatening to kill everyone on board before being overpowered in a gripping finale while flying over a mountainous region.

Plagiarised storyline – A sculptor is murdered on a

coach. Several people on board wanted him dead. The coach attendant, and her partner, the coach driver, turn amateur sleuths. During the five-hour trip and after much clever detective work, they deduce that the murderer is the co-driver, who hijacks the coach threatening to kill everyone on board before being overpowered in a gripping finale while hurtling down a twisting, mountainous road.

Plagiarism or breach of copyright?

It is neither plagiarism nor a breach of copyright to rework or develop other people's ideas. For example, if you are writing an article or book on any particular topic – from the meaning of flowers, to the Industrial Revolution – you will naturally consult books and documents written on that subject. Your work would be bound to contain similar facts, but should be written up, and presented, in your own unique way, and also include new material where possible.

It is not plagiarism or a breach of copyright to quote short passages from someone's work, as long as you acknowledge the original source. It should be clear that you are citing another author, and an appropriate reference should be given, including the title of the work, the year it was published and the publisher.

Publishing a work without the author's permission is a breach of copyright, even if the author is acknowledged. You may be allowed to reprint part of another author's work by gaining permission from the copyright holder. If it forms part of a book, it is usual to contact the publisher and its use will involve a fee.

To summarise:

• Plagiarism is presenting someone else's work as your own

- Using several research sources means you form your own views
- In fiction, it is plagiarism to follow another author's storyline
- It isn't plagiarism to rework, or expand on, another's ideas
- It isn't plagiarism to quote short passages, as long as you acknowledge the source

Point of View

See also: Consistency, Fiction, Final Checks, Teen Fiction

Have you chosen the point of view in which to tell your story and adhered to it? Be aware of the limitations of certain points of view, as any inconsistencies will be quickly spotted. In particular, if using a first person narrative, remember that you cannot credit your character with any knowledge of the action that takes place beyond his or her firsthand experience.

If using third person point of view, make sure you stay with the same character's inner thoughts throughout a scene. If possible, stay with the character for the entire chapter. If it is essential to show action, or point of view, from another character during a chapter, always signal to the reader at the opening of the next scene that you have done so.

When changing scene (and/or point of view) you should leave a line of white space before typing the first line of the new scene. Alternatively, you can insert asterisks between the final line of the old scene and the first line of the new one. The new scene starts with the writing blocked to the left (without indent).

To summarise:

- Choose the point of view for your story and stick to it
- First person viewpoint is limited and cannot include information it isn't possible for the central character to know
- Stay within one point of view for each scene
- If possible, keep to one point of view for each chapter

Preparation

See also: *Angles, Articles, Discipline – Staying on Topic, Markets, Research*

You've thought of a basic idea for a non-fiction article, but how do you go about writing it up so that an editor will want to buy it? Preparation is a key factor. Whatever the subject matter, a saleable article must have a focal point; it shouldn't wander away from its core theme, or have semi-related facts crammed in simply because it seems a shame not to include them.

Let's assume you've chosen to write about shoes. Give the blank page a heading, but don't get too hung up on what to call the article at this stage; a lot of time can be wasted on trying to think up a perfect title and you'll probably change it later anyway.

All successful writing has a focus, so the first step in preparing an article is to make a list of areas that could be covered.

For example:

- History – shoes through the ages
- Fashion – ideas that never caught on, or styles that go full circle
- Designer – shoes made with art, rather than

practicality, in mind
- Manufacture – how shoes are produced and the type of materials used
- Work – from clogs to ballet shoes
- Celebrity – well-known shoe addicts and their collections
- Health – feet problems caused by ill-fitting shoes
- Cost – the most expensive shoes ever
- Children – the importance of correctly fitting shoes

As this list illustrates, one topic can have any number of different angles. The entire subject of shoes is too wide, and would become too generalised to cover in one article, and so would be unlikely to find favour with any editor.

Choose the slant best suited to your target publication. A magazine aimed at young women isn't likely to be interested in the history of shoes, and a trade publication dealing in shoe manufacture will already be aware of how shoes are made, for instance.

Keeping in mind your intended market, the next stage in the preparation process is to tighten your approach so that it covers just one main area. Pick an idea from your first list and create a second list, brainstorming until you have plenty of relevant ideas to work on. This will flag up the necessary research. Don't be tempted to step outside your chosen focus – you can always use other standpoints to write different articles.

Finally, gather together all your newly acquired data and arrange it in a logical sequence. Now you're ready to write.

To summarise:
- Prepare a list of general areas your article idea might cover

- Choose a theme from this for a tighter approach
- Assemble your data into a logical sequence

Press Release

See also: *Books, Children's Picture Books, Publishers, ZZZZ – Sleep on It*

A press release is an effective way to get some free publicity. If your book has been taken on by a conventional publisher, its marketing department will deal with the publicity stories released to the media, but, for a self-published book, this task will fall to you.

A press release is circulated to local and regional newspapers and to any national magazines which have some relevance to the book's subject matter. There is no guarantee that any of the editors you contact will publish the story, but local press in particular are always on the lookout for stories concerning people in their community.

The function of a press release is to supply newsworthy, interesting, and pertinent information, so your story won't find favour if it comes across as a straightforward blatant advertisement for your new book.

Some publications will use your press release as the basis for a longer or shorter feature of their own. But you should take into account the fact that others will run it as it is – word for word. Because of this, you have to write your story as you would like to see it reported. This means keeping it concise, pithy, and error-free.

Editors receive many press releases. To ensure yours will be considered for publication, present it in a professional way by following the customary layout.

- Write in the third person
- Use double spacing

- Type the text in Times New Roman or Arial
- Keep it to one page, if possible

Write PRESS RELEASE in capitals and centre it at the top of the page. Below this, indicate when the release can be used. This will be the date when your book is available; if that is straight away, write 'for immediate use'.

Under this comes the all-important headline which should describe the content of the press release in a nutshell. Sharp, concise, and amusing headlines are the most attention-grabbing. Type in bold and centre it on the page.

The first paragraph contains a brief summary of what the press release is about and this is followed by more detail in consecutive paragraphs. Explain the book's theme in a few words, what inspired you to write it, and your interests and experience in the field. Keep the release lively by including a piece of information as a direct quote.

At the bottom of the page, write your contact details including a phone number and/or email address, so that you can be contacted immediately if the editor needs further information.

Print off some pictures of the book cover and a head and shoulders shot of yourself. Write a caption on a label for the back, and include with the editorial.

It's important to consider the timing of your press release. Magazines may not have space to include your editorial for several weeks, or longer, if it's a monthly publication. Local press, on the other hand, might be persuaded to run the story to coincide with a book signing, an appearance on local radio, or a talk or demonstration held locally.

To summarise:

- Be sure your story is newsworthy, not a blatant advertisement
- Write your press release as you'd like to see it reported
- Present your copy in the customary layout
- Give local press details of planned publicity events

Professionalism
See also: *Editors, Final Checks, Invoicing*

Editors like to work with professional writers, that is, writers who conduct themselves in a professional way. If you come across as an amateur, you'll sabotage any chance of seeing your work in print.

In publishing, deadlines are sacrosanct, so it's imperative to deliver work on time, or ahead of schedule, if possible. Take care to get it as good as it can be before you submit. Once the editor has your article, spotting errors or omissions, and having to send him corrections, looks unprofessional and could reflect badly on you.

Accept rejections with good grace. All writers are disappointed when their work is turned down, but, no matter how angry you feel when a rejection lands in your inbox, never fire off an irate email in reply.

Don't ask how much you'll be paid for writing a feature before it has even been commissioned. If your idea is accepted, you will be told the fee, and if you consider it isn't going to be worth your while, decline politely.

Keep your standards high and deliver your best work on every project, not just the better paid assignments. Situations within the publishing world change rapidly, and opportunities can arise for trusted freelances when editors have new projects in mind, or move on to magazines which have higher budgets.

Be patient, and don't hassle the editor for a response to a query the day after you've sent it.

Send in your invoice promptly, making a clear statement of the relevant details. Don't ask for payment on acceptance, if their usual practice is to pay on publication.

Emails:

Because it's easier and quicker to communicate electronically, there's a temptation to whisk off emails to our professional contacts in the same way we might to family and friends. But it's important to take the same care and attention when communicating with editors by email, as you would when writing and posting letters to them in the traditional way.

Do:

1. include your contact details on every email
2. use a standard font such as Times New Roman or Arial
3. use a spellchecker to pick up errors
4. proofread before sending, to pick up grammatical mistakes
5. use a blank line to separate paragraphs
6. ensure the subject line is explanatory and not spam-like

Don't:

1. write in coloured text
2. type entirely in capital letters
3. use smiley faces or acronyms like LOL
4. use abbreviated 'text speak'
5. send attachments without first checking with the recipient
6. be too informal and 'matey'

To summarise:

- Deliver material on time
- Don't talk money before being commissioned
- Ensure standards are high on every project
- Keep email communication businesslike

Proofreading

See also: *Capital Letters, Consistency, Edit, Final Checks, Punctuation*

A thorough examination of your text to find and correct typographical errors and mistakes in grammar, style, or spelling should always be undertaken before submitting for publication.

When you proofread your work, leave a decent period of time between finishing the writing and checking it. Putting it aside for a while means you'll come back to it having a fresh approach and picking up more errors.

It can help if you read your work out loud. Doing this highlights poor grammar and flawed sentence construction. It's also wise to print off a hard copy to proof, rather than reading straight from a computer screen, as this, too, will make mistakes easier to spot.

Take your time and proofread your work systematically, a little at a time. A good trick is to use a blank sheet of paper, or a ruler, to run down the page, as this keeps your eyes focussed on each line.

Check that apostrophes haven't been missed out and that those used are in the correct place. It's also very easy to miss words out altogether. You know what you meant to write, but have you left out the odd *and, the, it,* and so on? These omissions can be difficult to spot because our brains automatically add them in when we read a sentence.

Common 'typos' include getting letters the wrong way round. This is especially true of the letters 'i' and 'e' in words like 'receive' and 'belief'. If you write on a computer, use the spellchecker, but remember, although a spellchecker will point out many errors, it will ignore similar-looking, but misused, words like 'quite' and 'quiet'.

You are not only proofing the spelling, punctuation, and grammar; the whole document should be consistent. Look for unwitting variations in style and formatting, such as font size, line spacing, underlining, and headings. Double-check that the spelling of names has remained the same throughout, that Lynn hasn't become Lynne or Lyn later in the story.

It can be very helpful to get someone else to do a final proofing for you, as often she will pick up on things that you miss when checking your own work.

To summarise:
- Don't try to proofread without putting work away for a while
- Read your work out loud
- Print off a hard copy to proof
- Check for missing words
- Proof for inconsistencies in style and formatting
- Get someone else to read your work

Public Lending Right

See also: *Illustrations, Keeping Records*

Public Lending Right (PLR) is a government-funded scheme which makes payments to authors and illustrators whose books are borrowed from UK public libraries. You will need to register with the PLR office and payments due are calculated on the estimated number of times your book has been borrowed nationally. This estimated figure is taken from a sample of about thirty library authorities around the country; at least seven authorities are changed each year.

To qualify you do not have to be the copyright holder, but you do need to be named on the book's title page, or be entitled to royalty payments from the publisher.

Public lending right and co-authorship

For joint authors, the PLR will be divided between the collaborators. This might be a 50-50 split, or a different percentage share depending on creative input, but should be worked out before you register. The percentage share being agreed, each co-author must then submit a separate application. A co-author may only claim his or her own share even if the collaborator is deceased or does not wish to apply for Public Lending Right.

Authors who are eligible for PLR must, at the time of registering, have their main home in the UK or the EC Member States, or Norway, Iceland or Liechtenstein.

Details of how to register can be found on the PLR website or by contacting it by post.

Public Lending Right
Richard House
Sorbonne Close
Stockton-on-Tees
TS17 6DA

Tel: +44 (0)1642 604699
Fax: +44 (0)1642 615641
www.plr.uk.com

To summarise:

- Authors must first register for Public Lending Right

- Payment is calculated on estimated loans from UK public libraries
- Joint authors need to apply separately

Publishers – When and How to Approach Them

See also: Agents, Books, Covering Letters, Fiction, Layout and Formatting, Marketing, Preparation, Press Release, Research, Synopsis, Teen Fiction, Title Page, Word Count, X Factor, Yours Sincerely

Assuming you do not have an agent and wish to approach a publisher directly, there are certain things you need to do before submitting your manuscript.

The first, and most important, area to cover is researching the right publisher for your needs. Start by reading the *Writers' and Artists' Yearbook* and compile a list of all the publishers who cover your particular genre. Cross out all those who only consider submissions from agents. Study each publisher's details carefully. Go to its website, if one is available, to see what type of books it has on its list. If available online, read the detailed submission guidelines, or send away for them.

From your first list you should now have a shortlist of those most suitable to approach. Telephone each one and ask to whom your submission should be addressed and *exactly* what is required from you.

The following will give you a general idea of what to submit, but this will vary from publisher to publisher.

Fiction

The first requirement for fiction is to finish the book. Then put it away for several weeks, revise it until you are happy it is as near to perfection as it can possibly be, and only then look for an outlet for it. Never submit to a publisher unless you have the full manuscript, revised, rewritten and carefully edited line by line, available to send immediately it is asked for.

You would normally be expected to send as an initial submission:

- A covering letter addressed to the correct person
- A single spaced synopsis (one page is best, but, if this is not possible, keep it as brief as you can)
- The first three chapters, double spaced, and the pages numbered
- A self-addressed and stamped envelope for the reply and return of manuscript

Non-fiction

The submission requirements for a non-fiction book are completely different to a novel. In this case, it is better by far not to finish the book before submitting it, or, if you have, not to say so in your initial approach. A publisher who is interested in the basic idea may want you to deal with certain aspects in a different way to your outline. If you have already written the book, this could mean lots of wasted time and effort on your part, but, worse still, would be the publisher rejecting the proposal because he feels the completed work is not suitable for his list. Giving the publisher an outline of your intentions opens the door for dialogue that could well result in a publishing deal.

Covering letter:

You need a covering letter, as in the case of fiction, addressed to the correct person. The letter should start with a one-paragraph hook which encapsulates the essence of your idea. Briefly describe the target audience, the gap in the market, and say why you are the right person to write the book. Give the working title and estimated word count. Say whether the book would be illustrated. Include an addressed envelope with sufficient postage for the return of the proposal.

Proposal:

The proposal contains a title page, details of what your book is all about, including any unique selling points. State also how you intend to handle the subject matter. A section covering the competitors in the market place, a section on marketing aims, an author's biography, a table of contents, a chapter by chapter synopsis, and one or two sample chapters, depending on the publisher's requirements.

Title page:

This contains your contact details, the title of the work and word count.

Competition:

Say which books you see as competition and why your book will fill a niche not covered by any of them. Or, if your book is along very similar lines, state why yours is better. Never run your competitors' work down, simply stress where you feel yours is superior.

Marketing:

Give a detailed account of the prospective market and how you see your work tapping into that audience. You need to include details of how you will be able to help with marketing your material. Say which magazines you can write for, list local events, and suggest radio stations that could be approached to publicise your work as a local author. Include any information which shows your willingness to self-promote your work.

Biography:

Write this in the third person, and use it to establish your credibility, both as a writer, and as someone qualified on the subject.

Table of contents:
This shows how you intend to organise your material. Give a list of the chapters including titles and subtitles, if appropriate.

Chapter by chapter synopses:
Write a brief description of what each chapter will contain and try, where possible, to use the same tone as you have used in writing the sample chapters.

Sample chapter or chapters:
For a non-fiction book, it isn't always necessary to send the opening chapters.

Unless these are specifically requested, send the chapters you consider the strongest. Only send the number of chapters the publisher requires, having found this out by telephoning first.

To summarise:
- It is better not to have written the book before submitting a proposal for a non-fiction book
- The proposal is your sales pitch and needs to be strong
- Give the purpose of the book and show the tone you intend to take
- State why the book is needed
- Say why you are qualified to write on the subject
- Detail your target market
- Name competing titles and give reasons why your book is better
- List chapter headings
- Give a short synopsis of each chapter
- Unless the publisher requests opening chapters you can send the chapter or chapters you consider to be the strongest

Punctuation

See also: Dialogue, Grammar, House Style, Layout and Formatting

Apostrophes – misused and missing

If you are one of those writers who has trouble with the dreaded apostrophe, you can get to grips with it by following a few basic rules. The apostrophe has two functions – to show possession and to replace a missing letter.

To show possession:

An apostrophe is added before the letter 's' to denote possession.

My mother's garden: The garden that belongs to my mother.

Jane's car: The car that belongs to Jane.

The doctor's surgery: The surgery that belongs to the doctor.

The teacher's books: The books that belong to the teacher.

But, if you are writing about more than one doctor or teacher, the apostrophe is added after the plural.

The doctors' surgery: The surgery that belongs to the doctors.

The teachers' books: The books that belong to the teachers.

An apostrophe is also used to show possession in plurals that don't end in s

The people's choice

When a word already ends in 's' and has a z sound, a similar rule applies. The apostrophe is placed after the 's' – no extra 's' being needed.

Mr Jones' house

The business' phone number

But, *Jess's shoes*

An apostrophe is *not* used when indicating a straightforward plural.

Latest movies – not *latest movie's*

Special offers – not *special offer's*

To replace a missing letter:

An apostrophe can be used to indicate where a letter has been missed out of a word.

Isn't – is not

Wasn't – was not

Don't – do not

We're – we are

These contractions are often used in speech, or when you want to write in a less formal style.

However, if the missing letter comes at the beginning of the word it is necessary to make sure you have actually used an apostrophe and not opening quote marks.

I wasn't 'ere yesterday and **not** *I wasn't 'ere yesterday*

If the word begins a sentence then it must take a capital:

'Ere, what you doin'?

It's/its:

The rule that trips many people up is the one that applies to the words it's and its. It's is the abbreviated form of it is and it has and the apostrophe is used in place of the omitted letters 'i' and 'ha'.

It's a beautiful day: It is a beautiful day.

It's been a beautiful day. It has been a beautiful day.

This shows it's abbreviated: This shows it is abbreviated.

Remember, the apostrophe is only used here to replace a missing letter.

But an apostrophe is **not** used when writing about something that belongs to it.

The lorry shed its load

The dog is asleep in its basket

Colons

The colon is used to expand on the preceding sentence.

- There are many instances of Mozart's genius: at age
  six he wrote his first composition, at seven he had
  music published, and at age eight he composed his
  first symphony.

It introduces a list of items, which are then separated by
commas or semicolons.

- Students should bring the following: books, paper,
  pens and clipboard.
- The parade passed by: some floats carried singers;
  others had dancers; the brass band played; and
  laughing children ran behind.

Note that in the above examples what follows the colon
does not take a capital letter.

It introduces a quotation.

- Shakespeare said it best: "Neither a borrower nor a
  lender be." (Lord Polonius – *Hamlet*)

Commas

Commas have a variety of uses and this section will
cover the most common. If you are at all unsure about
basic grammar and punctuation we advise buying one of
the easy-to-follow guides available.

To separate words or phrases in a list:

Some house styles require a comma before 'and' if there
are three or more item in a list, others don't, but it is
important to be consistent in usage throughout a
document.

Phrases – On Thursday, Jack was fired, got mugged and
lost his car keys.

Nouns – He drowned his sorrows by drinking whiskey,
brandy and a beer chaser.

Adjectives – Afterwards he looked green, haggard, nauseous and tired.

The exception to the adjective rule is when the adjective is being modified.

Modified Adjective – His face had a pale green tinge.

Verbs – Jack was so upset he yelled, swore and muttered.

Clauses – Once he calmed down, which took some time, he was able to talk about his day, but his speech was slurred.

To enclose insertions:

Paris, home of the Eiffel Tower, is one of the world's beauty spots.

When using a participle to introduce a sentence:

Hoping to be the winner, Sarah entered the phone-in competition.

In tag questions:

You do love me, don't you?

We did arrange to meet tomorrow, didn't we?

When using interjections:

I would love some pie, thank you.

Please, won't you reconsider?

Yes, I did say that.

No, I didn't mean it.

When using a name in direct speech:

"Jack, are you still hung-over?"

"I'm telling you, Jack, you drink too much."

Incorrect punctuation can change the meaning of a sentence, so be sure your words say exactly what you want them to:

Jack loves you as a friend, I thought you should know.

Jack loves you; as a friend, I thought you should know.

Dialogue punctuation

Either single or double marks can be used, but it is

important to be consistent throughout the text. When the dialogue tag forms part of a sentence, you should use a comma after the speech, close the quote marks, and use a lower case letter for the tag.

"You drove me to it," he said.

Notice that in the examples below a lower case letter is used even when it follows a question mark or exclamation mark. This is because the tag is part of the sentence, not separate from it.

"How could you?" she asked.

"You're an idiot!" he yelled.

However, when no tag follows the dialogue you should use a full stop, question mark or exclamation mark to finish the speech and then close the quote marks.

"How could you?"

"Easily, you drove me to it."

"You're an idiot!"

When dialogue continues after the tag, **but is still part of the same sentence**, a comma is used, a lower case letter starting the next section of dialogue.

"There are times," she said, "when I could murder you."

When dialogue continues after the tag, **but is NOT part of the same sentence**, a full stop is used, a capital letter starting the next section of dialogue.

"I don't understand you," he said. "What on earth did you think you were doing?"

When speech continues over more than one paragraph do not use quote marks to close the paragraph, but do use quote marks to open the next paragraph. Insert a dialogue tag near the beginning of the following paragraph to show the reader the same person is still speaking.

Example: Jane stamped her foot. " ... and so I told Mary enough was enough.

"She didn't listen to me," Jane continued, "she never does."

Ellipsis

An ellipsis (…) shows that words or figures are missing from a piece of writing. Beginner writers often use more than three dots, but the correct punctuation is only three, no more and no less.

An ellipsis is often used with quotations. It usually appears in the middle or at the end of a quotation to show that not all of the quote has been used.

For example:

There were hundreds of writers, covering every genre and style of writing, at the symposium.

There were hundreds of writers … at the symposium.

It may be used at the beginning of a quote, but only if the quotation begins mid-sentence and what follows the ellipsis makes sense without the missing words.

The ellipsis can also be used to show a pause in a sentence and/or dialogue:

Sarah cried and cried … and then cried some more. "I wish I knew why …" she said.

When used mid-sentence, a space should be left between the first and last ellipsis marks and the surrounding words, but if a quotation tapers off (as in Sarah's dialogue above) you should leave a space between the last letter and the first ellipsis mark, but not between the last dot and the closing quotation mark.

If *words* are left off the end of a sentence, indicate the omission by ellipsis marks and then indicate the end of the sentence by a full stop …. But if one or more *sentences* are omitted, end the sentence before the ellipsis with a full stop followed by the ellipsis marks which should have a space on either side. …

When a quotation begins with a complete sentence and

ends with a complete sentence, it is not necessary to use an ellipsis unless it is important to emphasise that something has been omitted.

The plural of ellipsis is ellipses, but the dots themselves are called ellipsis marks or points.

Exclamation marks

Exclamation marks are nicknamed howlers and screamers by editors, publishers and agents because the novice writer tends to overuse them. They should be kept to an absolute minimum and only used if truly necessary.

They express exasperation, astonishment or surprise. They can also emphasise a comment or phrase.

Examples of usage:

Help! No! Go away! Stop! How extraordinary!

In dialogue you can use exclamation marks to show irony, but again, it is better to avoid them, and use the power of your characters rather than a screamer.

Examples of usage to denote irony:

'How kind you are!' – when the person addressed is anything but kind.

'He's such a gentleman!' – when the person described has acted in a non-gentlemanly manner.

If the sentence really needs an exclamation mark, and there are times when that is the case, then only ever use *one*. Ending a sentence with three or four is tantamount to begging the editor to reject your work.

Hyphens and dashes

It is important to understand the difference between a dash and a hyphen in a sentence.

A hyphen is used to join words together, such as: x-ray or ten-year-old. There is no gap between the words.

A dash is sometimes used in place of brackets in sentences which have parenthetical statements. For example: The characters in some novels – but certainly not all – leap from the page. A space is inserted between the words.

The decision on whether to use an 'en' dash (so called because it is roughly the size of the letter 'n') with spaces on either side or an 'em' dash (the size of the letter 'm') without spaces is often one of house style. Some publishers prefer one over the other.

To form an 'en' dash (on most keyboards), hold down CTRL while pressing dash, alternatively type the first number or word, then hold down the ALT key while typing 0150 using the numeric keypad, and then type the next word.

An 'en' dash with spaces can also be formed by typing the first word, adding a space and then putting in two hyphens, adding another space and then typing the next word. The computer should convert the two hyphens into an 'en' dash.

To form an 'em' dash (on most keyboards), hold down CTRL and ALT while pressing dash, alternatively type the first word, then hold down the ALT key while typing 0151 using the numeric keypad, and then type the next word.

An 'em' dash can also be formed by typing the first word, putting in two hyphens, and then typing the next word. The computer should convert the two hyphens into an 'em' dash.

When to use hyphens:

1.   To avoid confusion or ambiguity:

The number was recalled (the number was remembered)
The number was re-called (the number was dialled again)

2.   With numbers from twenty-one to ninety-nine

3. In fractions: two-thirds, five-ninths
4. To make a compound adjective:
A 90,000-word novel
A drug-addicted tramp
But note that compounds beginning with an adverb ending in 'ly' are not hyphenated. So it would be brightly lit and not brightly-lit.
It is also important to remember that an adjective preceding a noun is treated differently to a phrasal verb following a noun. A well-known actor opposed to an actor who is well known.
5. To avoid doubling up on vowels or trebling consonants: re-educate, cell-like
6. When a prefix is added: ante-natal, post-operative
7. Compound family relations: great-grandson, mother-in-law

When to use dashes:
The more informal the writing, the more acceptable it is to use a dash in place of brackets. In formal writing, brackets should be used.
You should never use dashes to replace commas, but you can use them to add a deeper pause than a comma provides.
For example: You always think you're so great – you're not.
For ranges, 'en' dashes and not hyphens are used: 1914–18 war, Appendices A–D

Quotation marks
There are two different types of quotation marks: single and double. Double quotation marks are now used less than they were in the past, but some magazines and publishers still favour them over the single marks. Always check the house style of your target market to see which they prefer.

Whichever marks you use for direct speech, you would then use the opposite quotation marks to quote 'speech within speech'.

Example:
'I'm praying Jack hasn't started drinking again. When he left this morning he said, "I'm going to the supermarket", but that was hours ago and he should have returned by now.'

The double quotation marks show that someone is being quoted word for word.

Other uses for quotation marks:

* Idiomatic expressions, for example: He was always referred to as a 'pain in the neck'. Note that when quotation marks are used in this manner the full stop or comma comes *outside* the marks.

* When quoting the title of a magazine article or short story: 'The Generation Game' in *Spanish Magazine*, March 2007.

Semicolons

The semicolon is used to join connecting phrases without having to use a conjunction (such as and or but).

It is also used to join two *complete* sentences into one when the two sentences are so closely related that using a full stop to separate them lessens the meaning or impact, as in this famous example by Dickens: *It was the best of times; it was the worst of times.*

A semicolon is also used when a sentence is extremely long, contains several clauses, and commas are no longer sufficient to enable the reader to make sense of it. When this happens, the semicolons indicate the more important pauses in the sentence. Wherever possible, this should be avoided. It is much better to rewrite the sentence, breaking it down into two or three shorter sentences.

Q

Queries

See also: *Articles, Covering Letters, Editors, Guidelines, Outlines, Photography, Research, Sidebars, Titles, Topics, Word Count, Yours Sincerely*

Some magazines' guidelines say to submit complete articles for consideration, but these are few and far between. The majority of magazines request a query in the first instance. A query is a way of telling the editor what you intend to write about. It should give the title of the piece, the word count, how many and what type of sidebars. It should also state whether you intend to supply photography (and in what form) to accompany the finished article.

As you can see, the query contains lots of information and this allows the editor to decide whether your proposal suits her immediate needs. If you have researched the market carefully, you should be able to gauge the preferred word count and style of article the magazine accepts.

A query saves writers from wasting time on articles that editors might reject. Sometimes a query will lead to a slightly altered article to that intended by the writer. This could be because the editor wants emphasis on different aspects, or a longer piece, or the same subject looked at from another point of view. If the complete article had been written and submitted a rejection would have been forthcoming. By sending a query, it opens a line of communication which could lead to commissioned work. The query letter should be accompanied by an outline showing how the writer intends to tackle the article.

Queries should never be sent for fiction, which works in completely the opposite way to articles. Send the finished story, having first checked the guidelines and read several copies of the magazine to ensure it is the type of story the editor wants, with a very brief covering letter giving details of any previous publishing success.

To summarise:

- A query presents the editor with all the information needed to decide whether or not to commission your article
- Querying first saves wasted writing time if the editor wants to change the focus of your idea
- A query letter should always be accompanied by an outline
- Fiction does not require a query letter beforehand and should be submitted as a completed piece

Quotes

See also: *Accrediting Sources, Articles, Capital Letters, E-books, Interviews, Legal, Websites and Blogs, Writing for the Web*

Quotes add interest and credibility to articles and non-fiction books. They can make a dull piece of writing more colourful by quoting the actual words used by the person named. Readers are better able to visualise the event and feel as though they are being put in touch with the speaker. This personal feel changes the tone, because the reader gains insights to an event as experienced by the people involved.

Be very careful when using quotes. A quotation reveals a great deal about the person speaking, emphasises points, and draws attention to certain aspects of his or her character. A writer's duty is to use quotes in context and not misrepresent someone's words. When people are quoted, their authority and credibility are placed on view for all to see, so choose carefully and responsibly.

Attributing quotes

- Whether the quote is direct or indirect, always attribute the person quoted.
- The attribution normally comes after the quote, unless it is necessary to make it clear from the outset who is speaking. For example, when quoting two different speakers, one after the other, the second quote should start with the attribution to avoid confusion.
- Make sure the words used in the attribution properly express what was meant and how it was said. Using 'said' is generally safe, but if the speaker is refuting a suggestion, or arguing, or anything else which colours the words, you should choose the verb accordingly.
- Remember that only the exact words used by the speaker are placed in quotation marks.
- If it is necessary to give an explanation of what was meant by the quotation, that explanation should precede the quote, so that the reader can better understand what is being said.
- Only quote when you fully understand the meaning.
- Identify the speaker by his full name and/or title the first time you quote him. Thereafter, use either his first or last name only, depending on the level of formality of the piece.
- If the quote is longer than one sentence, you should place the attribution at the end of the first sentence.
- Ask the person quoted to write her full name, or, if you have written it, ask her to check you have the

correct spelling.

Famous quotes

Quotes from renowned works, or words from famous people, even when the words are well known, should still be attributed.

Be careful when using famous quotes in your writing, as some quotes have been so overused they are in danger of becoming clichéd.

Pullout quotes

A pullout (or pull) quote is a section of text 'pulled' from the main body to stand out on the page as a teaser, or draw card, to entice the reader to find out more.

These are used frequently in magazines, but selecting them is usually the domain of the editorial staff. Once you have established a good working relationship with an editor, you could suggest pullout quotes from your text, but, for the beginner writer, it is best not to do so.

The exception to the above is when writing for the Web, or producing an e-book. If you are posting articles directly to a website, you should pick out interesting snippets to use in a box as a teaser for the main text.

"Pick out interesting snippets to use in a box." This is an example of a pullout quote taken from the preceding paragraph. The quote would be in a different colour, font and size to the main text, so that it attracted the eye of the reader.

If you are submitting an article to the editor of a website, it would be a good idea to submit a list of possible pullout quotes to accompany the text.

To summarise:

- Quotes add interest and credibility to an article, but the writer should use them responsibly
- Always attribute the quote

- Ensure the correct verb is used to show how the words were said
- Only direct quotes go inside quotation marks
- Some famous quotes can appear clichéd
- Pullout quotes are normally chosen by the editorial staff for print publications
- When submitting directly to the Web, or if writing an e-book, use pullout quotes to add interest to the page
- When submitting text to an editor of a website, include a list of suggested pullout quotes

R

Rejections

See also: Agents, Articles, Books, Editors, Feedback, Markets, Publishers, Revision and Resubmitting

Dealing with rejection is hard. But it is part and parcel of being a writer. There isn't a published writer anywhere on the planet that hasn't had work rejected. A certain Mr S. King, who is one of the most successful novelists of our age, claims he was once able to paper a room with his rejection slips. So, if your work is rejected, you'll be in good company.

It's what you do after rejection that is important to you as a writer. You need to use rejections in a positive way. If your manuscript comes back with a form letter saying it isn't right for the publisher's list, you need to look critically at how and why you chose that publisher in the first place. If your subject matter isn't suitable, then you've wasted its time, and a fair amount of your hard-earned cash in ink, paper and postage.

If you've researched properly, but still receive a 'not right for our list' letter, although it's hard, you have to accept it, and move on. Agents and publishers receive huge volumes of material every week and sometimes work is rejected without being read. It happens; as writers we have to be thick-skinned and live with it.

Sometimes editors reject perfectly good work because they have recently published something similar, or have a short story or article in the pipeline that is too close to your idea.

Any pointers as to why the manuscript, article, or short story, failed to make the grade should be acted on. Editors, agents and publishers are busy people. It is very rare for anyone to take the time to tell you what's wrong with your work, so treat this information with respect and revise accordingly. When the work has been revised to the best of your ability, send it out again, making sure you are targeting exactly the right market.

Whatever you do, don't fire off a letter, or email, explaining how wrong an editor was to reject your work. He didn't like it – end of story. Venting your spleen won't change his mind, but it might make you a powerful enemy in what is a very difficult profession.

To summarise:

- Rejection is a fact of life for all writers
- Did you target the correct market for your work?
- Is there anything in the rejection which will help you to improve your work?
- Resubmit after revision, having carefully researched the new target market
- Don't respond angrily to rejections

Research

See also: Accrediting Sources, Groundwork or Guesswork, Preparation

Tracking down the all-important nitty-gritty for a novel, non-fiction book, article, or details to include in a short story is a time-consuming pursuit that every writer hopes will reap worthwhile rewards.

Writers often view research in one of two ways: either they find it a chore, skimming the surface of their topic and failing to get meaningful results, or they get so carried away with the research that they don't get around to actually writing anything.

The key is to prioritise what is needed for a particular project, and list:

1. The information essential to the project
2. Where data is held – libraries, county archives, museums
3. People who could be interviewed

By concentrating on the chief areas, research can be broken down into practical and workable chunks.

Checking

How can you be sure which data is correct when different sources give conflicting information?

- Use more than one book if gathering information in this way. Look at the bibliographies to ensure the writers haven't taken their info from the same source, otherwise you might perpetuate inaccuracies
- When using the Internet, look for sites run by the associations, societies, and official fan clubs of the people, or subjects, you wish to cover, as these will have the most reliable data
- Transcripts of documents may contain errors so, whenever possible, look at the originals
- Use primary sources rather than secondary sources if you can. A primary source is the original, while the secondary is material which has been written using the original source in some way
- Gather the views of more than one expert to lessen the risk of biased data and personal opinion over facts
- Be careful when citing facts and figures from older material, as newer research may mean this has become obsolete

Sometimes even reputable sources differ on dates or measurements. Rather than risk citing what may be an inaccuracy, it's possible to be correct without being specific.

For example:
The church was built in the first quarter of the twelfth century
The limousine was twice the length of two average family saloons

Fact finding

County archives: This is where the parish records are kept, but local archives hold much more, including things like old newspapers, trade directories, maps, letters, photographs, diaries and reference books. There is no charge to view the records.

Archival documents online: More and more documents are becoming available online, making tracking down information easier. The *Access to Archives* database contains catalogues describing archives held locally in England and Wales – dates cover the 8th century to the present day. (www.a2a.org.uk)

Documents Online allows online access to The National Archives' collection of digitised public records, including academic sources, which are separated into several categories. (www.nationalarchives.gov.uk/documentsonline)

Museums: Specialist museums are the ideal way to discover more about people, skills, and industry. Costumes, armoury, toys, vehicles, and other exhibits can be examined up close, since many museums offer a hands-on experience. The information is detailed and accurate.

Libraries: As well as giving access to encyclopaedias, specialist books such as 'Who's Who', reference books, directories, newspapers, and books on every topic imaginable, many libraries hold archival or special collections of some kind. Most have websites, allowing computerised access to catalogues via the Internet.

Books: When writing about an era within the past few hundred years, read contemporary books to get a feel for the language and mannerisms of the times. For short stories, where an overview of a certain historical period is all that's needed, the children's section of your local library can be hard to beat. Books on how people lived cover the Romans, Tudors, Victorians, and dozens of others. These books, usually illustrated in colour, act as excellent visual guides to clothes, furniture, transport and so on.

Internet: It is unwise to use the Internet as your only source. Anyone can publish on the Web, so the information shouldn't be taken at face value, but should be treated with a degree of caution. It may appear that ten sources are in agreement about certain facts, but much that circulates on the Web is simply data copied from one website to another, inaccuracies and all. Always question the quality of information you find on the Internet before you use it in your writing.

To summarise:
- Prioritise research to make it more manageable
- Cite data from the websites of official bodies
- Use primary rather than secondary sources
- Make use of children's illustrated history books
- Treat information from the Internet with caution

Revision and Resubmitting
See also: Kill Fees, Rejections

When your carefully prepared work is rejected, it is very easy to feel like giving up, but don't do that, rather revise and resubmit to a new market. Before beginning your revision, you need to decide which magazine you are targeting and carry out some market research, so that the style and word count is right.

Fiction

There could be any number of reasons that your short story has been rejected. One of them could be simply that the magazine in question has more accepted stories than it has room to place in the immediate future. However, just in case there is something in the actual story that needs revising, we suggest you look carefully at the following areas before sending it out again.

Characters: Are the people inhabiting your story real, having believable motives and actions?

Plot: Does it make sense all the way through, and contain both conflict and tension?

Dialogue: Does it sound believable and aid character identification? Reading it out loud will tell you where it doesn't work.

Opening hook: Do the first few sentences grab readers so that they feel compelled to read on?

Ending: Does the story come to a satisfactory conclusion, tying up all the loose ends?

Non-fiction – commissioned

If a commissioned article is rejected, it is usual for the editor to tell you why.

She may ask you to rewrite the piece, changing and/or fixing the areas with which she has problems. If this should happen, don't argue, or get into an 'artistic' mood. She knows what her readers want to read and, if you want your work to be published, you must rewrite your article as requested.

If she doesn't ask for a rewrite, or give genuine reasons for rejecting (such as straying off topic, or not writing to the style and word count agreed beforehand), you should send an invoice for a kill fee. This is usually for fifty per cent of the fee for the complete article.

Non-fiction – sent 'on spec'

As in the case of fiction, it is possible the rejection has little to do with the quality of the piece, but just doesn't fit the editor's needs at that particular time. You should still look critically at the article and try to identify any weak areas.

- Did you target the correct magazine?
- Does your writing style match existing material?
- Did you keep to the word count required?
- Fix any problems that you find, but this time having a new market in mind.

Do not resubmit any material unless specifically requested by the editor. Usually, in this business, a no means no.

To summarise:

- Revise carefully and fix any problems you find
- Keep your new target market in mind during the revision process
- If asked for corrections, or a rewrite, comply wherever possible
- If an article was commissioned, but rejected without valid reasons, send an invoice for a kill fee
- Never resubmit unless requested to do so by the editor

S

Serial Rights
See also: *Editors, Invoicing, Keeping Copies, Kill Fees, Legal, Markets, Newspapers, Writing for the Web*

You own the full copyright to your work until you assign rights to a third party. These rights can be broken down into various components and sold. Each right can be sold, or assigned, separately, or you can sell the entire package of rights in one transaction.

All electronic rights
You are selling all rights in electronic format worldwide, which means you cannot even use the work on your own personal website, but you still retain print rights.

All Rights
Selling All Rights means exactly what it says and should only be done when justified by the fee received. You will be allowing the publisher to use your work in any format it chooses, whether it is print or electronic, without any additional payment. You keep the right to say you are the author, but lose all the other rights. This means you cannot publish, market, or perform the piece. The only way to reuse your work is to rewrite it in a completely different form, even if the facts remain the same.

Electronic archival rights
As in the case of exclusive and non-exclusive electronic rights, archival rights usually have a time period specified. These rights are normally non-exclusive, so you can have the same article archived on several websites and still sell non-exclusive rights elsewhere. However, do check the contract to make sure you

haven't given exclusive archival rights.

Electronic rights

These rights work in a similar way to print rights in that you have first electronic rights, which means selling the work for the first time in electronic format. Even if it has previously appeared in print form you are still selling first electronic rights. In practice, though, some editors will only offer to purchase reprint rights if the work has appeared in print.

Exclusive and non-exclusive electronic rights

This means selling all electronic (but not print) rights for a specific period of time. At the end of the time period, the rights revert to you. For non-exclusive electronic rights the editor is purchasing the right to keep your work on the publication's website for a specified period of time, but you are free to sell the work to other websites at the same time.

First serial rights

When you sell a print publication the right to publish your story, article, or poem for the first time, you are assigning it first serial rights for the country in which the item will appear. All other rights remain with you. So, if you sell the same piece to an overseas publication, you are assigning first North American serial rights, first Australian and New Zealand serial rights, or the rights for whichever country you have sold into.

Reprint (second serial) rights

Selling second serial rights means giving a publication the right to publish your work *after* the piece has already been published elsewhere. You must always state when you are offering reprint rights, as the magazine may believe it is buying first rights unless you do so. If you are able to locate several markets for reprint rights, you are free to sell your work as often as you wish, as reprint rights are non-exclusive.

Subsidiary Rights

A book publishing contract might contain a clause covering subsidiary rights. Subsidiary Rights cover a variety of rights such as (amongst others) anthology and quotation, Braille, computer game, film, video, audiotape, educational, translation, book club, foreign rights.

It is advisable to obtain legal assistance with book contracts. The Society of Authors offer their members a contract vetting service (see www.societyofauthors.org).

Print publications and their attitude to electronic rights: Many publishers will not accept first serial rights if your work has appeared online, even if only on your own personal website. For this reason, it is advisable to only put work on your site that has already been published in print format.

The other side of this equation is that some print publications are now asking for electronic rights, as well as first serial rights, without offering an additional payment. It is up to you to decide whether the prestige of the publication, and the payment offered, is sufficient to give up these rights without an increased fee.

To summarise:

- You own the copyright in your work and can assign rights to various publications
- First serial rights are given to the publication which brings out your piece for the first time
- Each country can be offered first serial rights in the same work
- Reprint rights can be sold as many times as you are

able to find markets, but the publication must be made aware that you are only offering reprint (second) rights
- All rights should only be sold if the fee covers the loss of income you will suffer from giving up second rights in the first country of sale, first rights in other countries, and all electronic rights
- Subsidiary rights often appear in book contracts
- Electronic rights come in various forms and you need to understand which rights you are selling

Sidebars

See also: *Articles, E-books, Guidelines, House Style, Markets, Outlines, Queries, Travel Writing*

A sidebar is the term for information relevant to an article, but which doesn't appear in the main text. For example, when writing a travel article, the details of how to get to a town, or other information pertinent to the reader, such as the tourist office address and opening times would go in a sidebar.

These details appear to the side of the main text, usually in a box, to draw attention to the information. Sidebars can also contain quotes, polls and lists related to the article.

Information which is not connected to the actual text, such as a table of contents, is not considered a sidebar.

The term is used in both newspapers and magazines and is also now common in web design, where sidebars are used to make links stand out more readily against the text.

Sidebar facts should be given to the editor on a separate page and clearly marked as additional information for the article you are submitting.

Most articles are enhanced by the use of sidebars. It is a good idea to mention in your query letter the information you intend to include.

To summarise:

- A sidebar gives information, directly related to the text, in small chunks
- Additional facts, not related to the text, are not considered a sidebar
- Clearly mark a separate sheet with the title of the article and the words 'additional information'
- Mention in your query the type of information you intend to submit as sidebars

Spelling and Grammar – Common Errors to Avoid

See also: *Consistency, Final Checks, Grammar, Proofreading, Punctuation*

Once again, we cannot stress strongly enough the need for a basic book on grammar. Also, if spelling is not your forte, use a good dictionary to check the usage of words. The list below covers some of the basic errors which signal amateur status to an editor.

As/like: Like is used before a noun – They looked **like** giants. **As** is used before a verb, or a clause containing a verb – **As** I feared, the weather was awful.

Here/hear: Here is the shop; **here** is the dog; **here** is the reason. **Here** is the opposite of there. **Hear** is a verb. We **hear** someone speaking; we **hear** rumours. Members of parliament shout: **hear, hear** – meaning I have heard and I agree.

I/me: To decide which of these to use take the other person out of the sentence and see which makes sense. (Maureen and) **I** write for a living. The contract was written for (Maureen and) **me**.

Lay/lie: **Lay** (put somewhere) those papers on the desk (past tense is laid). I'm going to **lie** (in a horizontal position) down, but (just to confuse the issue) the past tense of lie is lay.

Less/fewer: An easy way to remember this one is if you can count it, or divide it, you use fewer; otherwise you should use less. There was **less** sugar in the bowl (you cannot count sugar) than yesterday. There were **fewer** cubes of sugar in the bowl (you can count the cubes of sugar) than yesterday.

Lets/let's: The word **lets** (having no apostrophe) has many uses: Mary **lets** John stay. The landlord **lets** the apartment. **Let's,** having an apostrophe, has only one use – it means **let us** and the apostrophe replaces the missing 'u': let's go to the shops.

Loose/lose: If the collar is **loose** (not tight enough) you might **lose** (mislay) the dog.

Of/have: Never use **of** when you mean **have**. She **should have** gone to work. He **could have** left early. They **would have** preferred to holiday abroad. If these are contracted they become: She **should've** gone to work. He **could've** left early. They **would've** preferred to holiday abroad. **Never, never, never**: should of, could of, or would of.

Practice/practise: **Practice** is a noun and **practise** is a verb. John **practises** medicine at his **practice**. Don't forget to **practise**. Don't forget to do your **practice.** A friend of ours always remembers the rule by reminding herself that ice is a noun – so **practice** (ice) is also a noun.

There/they're/their: **There** is a way to remember the correct use of these. **They're** (they are, the apostrophe replaces the missing 'a') easy to get right if we think about **their** (possessive) uses.

To/two/too: Two is a number – **two** cars, **two** people, or **two** books. Working out the difference between **to** and **too** might be harder. Perhaps the easiest way to remember it is **too** means 'as well'. I'm going, **too** – this means I'm going as well (in this context, the **too** normally needs a comma before it although some publishers now prefer not to use a comma before **too** and **though** at the end of a sentence). **Too** is also used to denote excess: too much, too little, too often. I'm going **to** (go somewhere or do something) the park or the shop (both nouns) or to work, to run, to write (verbs).

Welfare/farewell: When you are concerned with someone's **welfare,** only one 'l' is required, but, when saying **farewell** to someone, the 'l' doubles up – imagine both hands waving.

Then/than: He has more work **than** I have, but when I have finished writing, **then** I can help him.

Who/whom: Who replaces the subject of the sentence. He is missing the point – **who** is missing the point? **He** is.

Whom replaces the object; this means **whom** replaces him, her or them. You also use **whom** when it follows a preposition, such as: for, to, or with. For **whom**; for **him**. To **whom**; to **her**. With **whom**; with **them**.

Who's/whose: Who's (who is, who has, the apostrophe replaces the missing 'i' or 'ha') going to take the books? taken the books? **Whose** (possessive) books are they?

Your/you're: As in other examples, one is a possessive and the other a contraction – it is **your** (possessive) duty to learn the difference; **you're** (you are – missing 'a' replaced by apostrophe) going to find it easy.

Synopsis

See also: *Agents, Books, Covering Letters, Fiction, Guidelines, Layout and Formatting, Publishers, Teen Fiction, Yours Sincerely*

Even established writers dread writing synopses, so it stands to reason that beginner writers are going to struggle, unless they have some guidelines to follow.

Fiction

You do not need a title page for the synopsis, your contact details go in the covering letter, and the novel's details go on the same page as the synopsis. Start by putting the following information in the top left-hand corner of the page.

Name:

Title:

Word Length:

Genre:

Or, if writing for children, put: Genre and age group:

You can write the synopsis either before you write your novel, or after, but, as you should never submit fiction to an agent until the entire novel is written, this section will deal with writing a synopsis for a completed work.

Layout and formatting:

Use single line spacing and try to condense the synopsis to a single page. Block the first paragraph to the left and indent all subsequent paragraphs. Write **only** in the present tense, using the third person. Each time you introduce new characters, put their names in capitals, but revert to lower case thereafter.

Write the synopsis in the same style as the novel. If humorous, use humour in the synopsis. If the book is a rollercoaster thriller, then so should the synopsis be. Open with a hook which will grab the reader.

You do not have to mention every character in the book, but you must include all the important ones. Similarly, you do not need to detail every twist and turn of the plot, but you must show clearly what the book is about, the highs and lows of the story, what is at stake for the main characters, and how the heroes deal with the plot shifts. Do make sure the storyline follows a logical sequence and comes to a satisfactory conclusion. **Always** give the ending of the novel. Apart from anything else, this shows the agent you have worked through the plotline and ironed out any hitches.

Make the synopsis come alive by writing with feeling. This is a condensed account of your novel, and you need to lavish as much care on it as you did on the full length version.

To summarise:

- Use present tense
- Open with a hook
- Clearly define main characters and conflicts
- Make your characters sympathetic, so that the reader will care about them
- Include the ending
- Check for spelling, grammar and punctuation errors

Non-fiction

Although a novel should be written before submitting a synopsis to a publisher, for non-fiction, the exact opposite is true. Not only is it unnecessary to have written the book, it may even work against you if you have. Often a publisher will suggest a change of direction or emphasis. If the book has already been written, this could mean you lose out on the deal or, at best, have to rewrite it.

You should, however, have written the first chapter, as

the publisher is quite likely to want you to submit a sample of your writing. This is a safeguard on the publisher's part, to ensure you can write and also assess the tone you are intending to take.

The synopsis for a non-fiction book is more like a sales pitch and must grab interest from the outset. State the book's proposed purpose, why you feel there is a need for it, what makes you qualified to write on the subject, your target market, any competing titles and why your book will be better. Include a working title, and a list of chapter headings with a brief outline of the points covered under each chapter.

This subject has been covered in greater detail under Publishers – When and How to Approach Them.

T

Teen Fiction
See also: *Agents, Books, Fiction, Layout and Formatting, Publishers, Synopsis, Yours Sincerely*

Age
The teenage market encompasses everything from pre-teen to young adult interest. Publishers are aware that readers of eleven or twelve devour teen fiction, while books aimed at the older end of the age scale are marketed specifically as Young Adult (YA).

Crossover books
These are novels that publishers have identified as having appeal for both the children and the adult market and are promoted to both. They can appear as separate editions and are sometimes marketed with different cover designs.

The bestselling novel, *The Curious Incident of the Dog in the Night-time* by Mark Haddon is a prime example of a successful crossover book.

Theme
Whatever your chosen theme, remember that books targeted at the teen market should have a teenage protagonist and a storyline typically consistent with the age and experience of the central character.

Subjects that may once have been considered taboo are acceptable if written with sensitivity. Often described as 'issue' based, these books include such topics as bullying, divorce, drugs, illness and teenage pregnancy.

But books for teens don't have to be gritty or edgy; many top-selling novels cover lighter themes, so choose something which appeals to you as an author. Popular fiction genres include humour, mystery, fantasy, historical, romance, adventure, horror, and sci-fi as well as stories that reflect the lives of today's teenagers.

Language

Although speech patterns in dialogue should be up-to-date, it's a mistake to try to write deliberately like a teenager, or what you believe a teenager sounds like. What is 'cool' when you begin your novel will be 'totally sad' by the time it's published – and probably even before you've reached the final page and typed The End. Swearing, provided it isn't gratuitous, is usually acceptable in YA books.

Length

Alongside the huge variation in readership age and subject matter, the length of books aimed at the teenage and YA market can vary enormously. A good average would be 30,000 to 45,000 words.

To summarise:

- Your main character should be a teenager
- Choose a genre that appeals to you
- Don't try to write like a teenager

Tense

See also: *Dialogue, Grammar, Point of View, Proofreading*

Tense involves an implied time-frame in which the action of a story takes place. Shifting the tense unnecessarily, or unwittingly from past to present to future, can be confusing for the reader. Be careful not to shift from one tense to another when the time-frame should be the same.

For example:

Incorrect: The writer **turns** from the computer, **stared**

out of the window, and **wishes** inspiration would strike.

Present: The writer **turns** from the computer, **stares** out of the window, and **wishes** inspiration would strike.

Past: The writer **turned** from the computer, **stared** out of the window, and **wished** inspiration would strike.

It is fine to shift tense to indicate a change in time-frame from one action or situation to another.

For example:

The editor **loves** (present) the new book, which he **accepted** (past) for publication. **Loves** is present tense, referring to a current situation; **accepted** is past, referring to an action which took place before the current time-frame.

When we tell a friend about our holiday, or even what we did a few moments ago, we use past tense because we're relating something that has happened – in other words, we are storytelling. The majority of short stories and novels are written in past tense because it is the most natural way for us to share a story.

For example:

By the time Robert **became** aware of the waiting taxi, the car horn **had** been **sounded** five times. Robert **had been arguing** with his girlfriend on the phone. He **slammed** down the handset, **stood** up, and **ran** a hand through his untidy hair. Outside in the lane, the taxi driver **drummed** the steering wheel impatiently.

Writing in the present tense gives a short story or novel a more immediate feel but can be tricky to maintain for any length of time.

For example:

By the time Robert **becomes** aware of the waiting taxi, the car horn **is sounding for the fifth time**. Robert **is arguing** with his girlfriend on the phone. He **slams** down the handset, **stands** up, and **runs** a hand through

189

his untidy hair. Outside in the lane the taxi driver **drums** the steering wheel impatiently.

Non-fiction articles are generally written in the present tense unless they involve a historical event. Quoted passages are also alluded to in the present tense.

Incorrect: The famous opening line of Daphne du Maurier's *Rebecca* **was** 'Last night I dreamt I went to Manderley again'.

Correct: The famous opening line of Daphne du Maurier's *Rebecca* **is** 'Last night I dreamt I went to Manderley again'.

Basic rules of verb tense

Simple forms:

Present = write/s

Past = wrote

Future = will write

Continuous forms:

Present = am/is/are writing

Past = was/were writing

Future = will be writing

Perfect forms:

Present = has/have written

Past = had written

Future = will have written

Perfect continuous forms:

Present = has/have been writing

Past = had been writing

Future = will have been writing

Examples:

Simple present: Chris writes a story.

Present continuous: Chris is writing a story.

Present perfect: He has written for most of his life.

Present perfect continuous: He has been writing for most of his life.

Simple past: Derek wrote a book last year.

Past continuous: Derek was writing a book last year.

Past perfect: He had submitted his book to several agents.

Past perfect continuous: He had been submitting his book to several agents.

Simple future: She will read my submission.

Future continuous: She will be reading my submission.

Future perfect: She will have read my book in three months.

Future perfect continuous: She will have been reading my book for three months.

To summarise:

- Be careful not to change tense unwittingly
- You can shift tense to indicate a change in time-frame
- Most short stories and novels are written in past tense
- Writing in present tense feels more immediate
- Non-fiction articles are often written in present tense

Theme

See also: *Fiction, Guidelines, Markets, Teen Fiction*

In fiction, the story being told is the plot, but underlying the plot is the theme of the story. For example, in science fiction novels, the plot is about characters and their experiences in an alien world, but a recurrent theme in such novels is the conflict between science and human nature.

The theme gives the plot depth. Whether you are writing a novel or a short story, you should decide on the theme running through your work and develop it.

The best way to decide on the theme is to reduce it to one sentence. If you look at many of Dickens' novels, the themes run along the lines of: the disadvantaged triumphing at considerable emotional cost to themselves and others. The plots are all different, but the theme is very similar.

When writing for the magazine market, the theme becomes very important. Literary magazines are unlikely to be interested in mainstream romance, but if there is an underlying theme of triumph over a natural catastrophe (earthquake, tsunami, volcanic eruption), they might feel differently.

For the women's market, the underlying themes need to be those their readers will identify with. What they want is to read about someone who feels real to them, dealing with a difficult situation, but overcoming her problems in the end. It's still a theme of triumph over adversity, but set within a plot that suits the market.

To summarise:

- The theme gives the plot depth
- Decide on the theme for your work and develop it according to the market
- You should be able to sum up the theme in one sentence

Title Page

See also: *Agents, Editors, Publishers*

The title page – also called a cover sheet – is an indispensable aid to book, short fiction and non-fiction manuscript presentation and is used for several reasons.

- It shows the editor, at a glance, what the manuscript contains
- It keeps the first page of your chapter, story, or

article clean
- It has your full contact details

There is no right or wrong way to present the title page, but it is important that it should be neat and clear, and contain all the vital information. The Serial Rights details should be included for short stories and articles, but omitted for books.

---

12 Writer's Way
My Town
MT12 3AB
Tel: 01234 987654
Email: me@publishedwriter.co.uk   31 May 2007

How to Make a Good Impression

By

Joanne Bloggs

First British Serial Rights   Word count: 2,000

Titles

See also: Legal, Markets

It's a truism that first impressions count. This is why choosing a good title is so important. The title of your work is the first thing the editor will read and, if it doesn't grab her attention, she may put down your submission in favour of one more intriguingly titled.

Articles

Not only does the title need to spark her interest, but it must also be a fair indication of what your non-fiction article is about. Your readers – and remember, the editor is your first reader and the one you need to impress – will have certain expectations based on what you've called your piece. A title should aim to sum up the point of your article, while tempting the reader to read on.

Your market research will have told you the sort of titles used by the publication you intend submitting to. Most magazines prefer fairly short ones, believing overly-wordy titles turn readers off. Some editors like a witty play on words, while others want titles to be more straightforward and descriptive.

Whatever you do, don't be boring or unoriginal. *What I Did on My Holiday in Wales* isn't going to stir any editor on a wet Monday morning and *Wales: Land of My Fathers* has been so overused that it's probably appeared on every editor's desk at some time or other.

Even after thinking up something you believe is perfect, a title is still subject to editorial change. The editor might want a different title for a number of reasons: she thinks her choice would better suit your article or the magazine's style, it's recently run an article which had a similar title, or perhaps she just doesn't like it.

Because the editor may choose an alternative, many writers consider their title to be nothing more than a 'working title'. Don't be too precious about it, but, at the same time, don't leave it solely to the editorial staff to come up with something suitable. Make sure your title piques the editor's interest sufficiently to ensure she reads your work in the first place.

Books

The choice of title for a book is even more important and, along with the book jacket, acts as a hook to ensnare potential buyers. Pick something distinctive, but easy to remember. Be aware of words that can be spelled a number of different ways, as potential buyers or booksellers may not easily find your book in catalogue listings.

Although the main title should carry the weight, subtitles are useful marketing tools for non-fiction books. The subtitle gives added information and explains how the book will help the reader. Book titles are also subject to editorial change, although the final choice is likely to be a mutual decision between you and your publisher.

Short stories

In the case of a short story, the editor may change your original title because she feels yours is too obscure. It may have some deep, or cryptic, meaning to you, but would pass over the heads of most readers. Or perhaps your title gives too much of the plot away as in: *Joan Marries her Childhood Sweetheart* – hardly worth reading on really, as we already know what happens.

To summarise:

- A title should sum up the point of your article
- Most magazines prefer fairly short titles
- Don't be boring or unoriginal in your choice
- Titles are subject to editorial change
- Some story titles give away too much of the plot
- Make sure your title piques interest

Topics

See also: Articles, Guidelines, Interviews, Markets,

Choosing the topic for an article is only the beginning of the process. The way the topic (or subject) is dealt with will depend on the target market. Let's say you decide to write about anorexia; this is the topic. Unfortunately, simply sending a query to an editor asking for a commission to write about anorexia will invariably bring a negative response. You need to decide how you will be handling the topic, before framing your query letter.

- The teen magazine market might be interested in anorexia as it affects their peer group. So, try to gain an interview with a famous role model who has recovered from, or is still affected by, anorexia. Similarly, taking a poll of a particular age group and presenting facts and figures of how widespread the problem really is, and how teenagers are coping with the pressure to diet, could pique the editor's interest.

- Weekly real life magazines would expect an entirely different approach. For this market, you would need to pitch the story of an ordinary person who has either beaten the problem, or been destroyed by it. The more sensational the story, the greater the chance of getting it accepted. The subject of the piece would also have to agree to photographs of her appearing in the magazine, preferably before, during, and after her battle.

- The magazines for slightly older women might require a more thoughtful approach. They would be more inclined to look at the influence (good and bad) celebrities have on young girls as well as the way in which the fashion industry manipulates how women see themselves, compared to ultra-thin catwalk models.

- Magazines aimed at the grey market, such as *Saga*, might be interested in an article on the subject as it affects their grandchildren.
- As you can see, choosing the topic is only the first step. Deciding how to pitch your query depends entirely on the target magazine, but always aim for an original approach, wherever possible.

To summarise:
- Deciding on the topic is only the first step
- Develop the topic according to the readership of your target market
- You can use the same research material to produce several different articles

Travel Writing
See also: Photography, Sidebars

Visiting new places, and getting paid for the privilege, appeals to a great many writers, so competition in the travel magazine market is fierce. Getting work accepted is by no means impossible, but editors do have very definite ideas of what they want to see in a travel article submission.

Before you book your ticket or set foot out the door, it's wise to research your chosen destination. Some pre-knowledge of the region, culture, or customs will enable you to write with more conviction, even if you don't use this information in your final piece.

Be selective
Don't try to cram a whole city or area into one travel article. Use a specific theme – the art galleries of Rome, or the gardens of Lisbon, for example. Pieces that focus on specific topics in this way can be written for

specialist magazines, or trade publications, which cover the subject matter, as well as for travel markets.

Decide on an angle

The angle is not the place you are visiting, but the way in which you present that particular destination. Editors are always looking for something which has an interesting slant such as a cooking holiday in France, wine tasting in Australia, cycling in Yorkshire, walking in Spain, painting in the Cotswolds, and so on.

Pictures – take lots of them

Some travel markets don't pay any extra for photographs, as they are considered to be part of the complete package. Writers' guidelines will indicate the preferred picture format for your chosen market but you might want to hedge your bets and take standard pictures (prints or transparencies) and digital ones.

Vary your pictures:

1. Be aware of colour and include plenty in your pictures
2. Don't just snap the well-known tourist sites and endless views of the beach
3. Take natural, rather than posed, photographs

Remember the human factor

Talk to the local people, ask questions, be curious. Humour is always a plus factor, but never poke fun at other cultures, or the way people speak. Add the occasional snatches of dialogue to bring the article to life and ensure it doesn't read like an entry in a guidebook.

Supply plenty of detail

Lack of essential detail is one of the main reasons otherwise good travel pieces get rejected. Keep a notebook with you at all times. Jot down addresses, phone numbers, access and amenities for wheelchair users or people with small children. You should also note opening times and entrance charges for museums, amusement parks, gardens, and theatres, and the prices of meals, snacks, and drinks. This information will appear in sidebars next to your main article and the editor will expect you to supply it.

Use all your senses

Visual descriptions are important, but don't forget sounds, smells and tastes. A good travel piece should show, not tell. Keep your eyes open for anything out of the ordinary – local rituals and customs add colour to a travel article. Just about everywhere in the world has been written about before, so think up new ways to describe the scene. Avoid using clichés; editors hate them. Don't give them 'quaint villages', 'bustling marketplaces', or churches that 'cling to mountainsides'.

To summarise:

- Have a particular angle in mind
- Look out for anything out of the ordinary
- Never poke fun at other cultures
- Use dialogue in your article
- Play safe and use a standard and a digital camera
- Make notes of prices, addresses and other details

Typing

See also: *Computers, Keeping Copies, Layout and Formatting, Letterheads*

Editors and publishers will no longer consider handwritten submissions, so manuscripts, proposals, queries and cover letters should always be typed.

You don't need to be an expert typist – a good many writers do very well using only two fingers. And, of course, there is nothing preventing you from writing in longhand first, if you feel you work better this way, as long as the final manuscript is typewritten.

If you work on a basic typewriter, use black typewriter ribbon and replace it as soon as the type begins to look faint. As you should keep a copy of each piece of work, you will need to either use carbons, or photocopy your manuscript, before sending the original – top copy – to an editor.

Electric typewriters at the higher end of the range will have some word processing features, but these machines can be similar in price to a computer.

Computers have several distinct advantages over basic typewriters:

- Spelling errors can be amended without the use of messy correction fluid
- Text can be revised and rearranged easily by cutting and pasting
- Work can be saved to a hard drive, or a disc, which means fresh copies of a manuscript can be printed off for each new submission

The only exception to the typewritten rule is when submitting a readers' letter to the letters page of a magazine. Editors of these pages are looking for letters from genuine readers, so don't type them on headed paper which advertises the fact that you are a freelance writer.

To summarise:

- Editors and publishers won't consider handwritten manuscripts
- Use black typewriter ribbon and replace regularly
- If using a typewriter, submit the original, top copy
- Computers are the most versatile option
- Don't type readers' letters, nor use headed paper

U

Unbiased Opinions

See also: *Articles, Final Checks, Markets, Opinion Pieces, Point of View, ZZZZ – Sleep on It*

An opinion piece is the only time writers should present work from their own point of view, but it is rare that an unknown writer has the luxury of writing opinion pieces. If you want regular sales, your writing should be as unbiased as possible. Keep your personal opinions hidden, and strive to present the facts without any partiality creeping in.

It is possible your writing might be coloured by your own personal beliefs without you being aware of it. Putting the piece away for at least two weeks before reading it again with fresh eyes makes it easier to review it objectively. If you spot any flag-waving or soapbox preaching coming through in your words, you must edit strenuously. If you don't, the editor will, always assuming she accepts the piece in the first place. She most probably won't accept it if it seems likely her magazine is being used to beat your own emotional, political, or lifestyle drum.

To summarise:

- Keep your beliefs and political views out of your writing
- To ensure you don't inadvertently present biased opinions, put your work away and then look at it objectively

V

Vanity Publishers

See also: Biography, Books, Publishers

Books

Because of the difficulties in today's publishing climate, self-publishing is becoming more common. This is an option many writers are taking up, but do be selective if you decide to go down that path. There are companies who prey on new and inexperienced writers, encouraging them to part with huge sums of money to see their work in print. The quality of the writing doesn't matter; neither does the question of whether or not the work stands any chance of commercial success. These predators praise the writing and promise that, for a considerable fee, the book will be printed, promoted and distributed.

Unfortunately, the resulting book is often poorly produced, and the writers find themselves not only considerably out of pocket, but they also have to find a home for boxes and boxes of unwanted books.

It is highly unlikely that your novel is perfect and without flaws, regardless of how often you have rewritten it, so if someone is over-enthusiastic, and praises it to the skies without pointing out any areas which still need work, do be wary.

There is nothing wrong with self-publishing, but it is difficult to distinguish between those who make their money purely from preying on authors' desire to see their work in print and those publishers who will assist you to produce something you can be proud of.

A brilliant website to visit is: www.vanitypublishing.info where you can get an advice pack if you are thinking of self-publishing.

Do remember that, because vanity presses are not selective, publication doesn't confer the same prestige as mainstream publishers.

Poetry

Although there are some excellent poetry competitions, unfortunately some are run on vanity publishing lines. These competitions accept just about anything that is submitted and the companies make their money from selling the resulting anthologies to the unsuspecting authors. From the point of view of presenting future work to an editor, there is little to be gained from mentioning you have had poetry published in one of these anthologies. Generally, if you have to pay to see your own work in print, it is quite likely to be a vanity publishing scam.

To summarise:

- Check that your potential publisher is genuine and not a vanity publisher
- If you are asked to pay to see your poetry in print, be wary
- Editors are not impressed by writing credits based on vanity poetry anthologies

W

Websites and Blogs

See also: *Biography, Clips, Nom de Plume, Queries, Serial Rights, Writing for the Web*

A writer's website serves many functions. It promotes the writer's work, establishes credibility, and provides an easy-to-access facility for editors to check on the writer's style and ability, but, most of all, it shows you are serious about your craft.

In today's world, writers are expected to have a web presence. Fortunately, it is relatively easy and inexpensive to produce one. The basic steps for producing a website or blog are set out below.

Blogs

More and more writers are using blogs to promote themselves. There have been some major book deals as a result of writing blogs, but these are rare. A blog is a less professional and more informal way of presenting your writing skills. If you consider the number of blogs currently on the Web, and compare that to the few blog-writers who have clinched a publishing deal, you'll realise the chances of a blog making your fortune are about on a par with scooping the main prize in the lottery.

So what exactly is a blog and how does it differ from a website? The term is an amalgam of the words web and log. A blog is an online journal for posting your views, work, pictures, or anything else you choose to share with humanity at large.

Journal entries, in reverse chronological order, are used to discuss whatever blog owners feel is important to them and often there is a facility for others to add to the blog. There are usually options to post writing samples and photography. However, if you are looking to impress editors, agents and publishers, unless your blog is unique and marketable, it is most probably better to have a website to promote your writing skills and keep the blog as something you share with like-minded people.

Domain names

You can use your own name (www.imawriter.com), or something relative to your particular area of expertise (www.joeblogspoetry.com). If you write under a name other than your own, you should use that for your website. Once you have bought your domain name, it is unique to you.

Finding a website host

The web host is where your website is stored on the Internet. Many service providers give web space to their clients as part of the package, together with a website wizard for easy building. If you lack technical abilities, that could be the easiest way for you to get started.

If you decide to go outside your service provider for a website host, an online search will produce plenty of alternatives.

Promote yourself

Insert your web address on emails, business cards and letterheads. Submit your site address to search engines. Have a links page, because the more pages you are linked to, the higher your site appears on searches.

Simply tasteful

The site is there to show off your writing skills, not to dazzle with graphics and fancy fonts. Keep it simple. You should have a home page, a biography page and links to samples of your work. On every page you should have an email link, so that it is easy for people to contact you directly from your website. The sample pages are very useful when querying by email, as you can include a link to your website in place of sending clips.

Do be selective in the choice of material to put on your website. It needs to be as professionally presented, as if you were submitting it to an editor. Check spelling and grammar for errors and correct them straight away.

Another point to bear in mind is that some editors feel anything appearing on the Web, even on a personal website, counts as published, so don't include anything for which you hope to find a market one day.

If your website host doesn't include a wizard to guide you through the web building steps, it is worth asking for professional help.

Writing is a business

By developing your website pages, you'll learn how to write for the Web, which is another skill you can use in your writing life. Although writing for the Web doesn't always pay as well as print publications, it adds more to your professional CV and experience.

To summarise:

- A website promotes the writer's work, establishes credibility and provides an easy-to-access facility to check on the writer's style and ability
- A domain name should contain your name and/or the type of writing in which you specialise
- Some editors consider work on a website as published, so don't post anything on your site that you still wish to sell
- Promote your website address on emails and stationery
- Add a links page and link to other sites

- A blog is a less formal type of web exposure and could be used as an alternative to a personal website, but anything crude or shoddy could detract from your projection as a professional writer

Writing for the Web

See also: Biography, Photography, Queries, Serial Rights, Websites and Blogs

Your chances of getting work published are even greater if you consider online markets. Almost all print publications have websites which have content that complements their conventionally produced edition and some use different content in their online magazine. There are also many hundreds of publications that exist solely as online enterprises.

Is writing for the Web any different from writing for print publications? The answer is 'most definitely', because people read web pages in a different way to a print publication. They scan the page, rather than read it word by word, and home in on certain words and sentences. This means web writing needs to be presented in a particular way.

Paragraphs should be short – no large blocks of text, and having just one point made per paragraph. The tone is generally friendly and conversational, rather than formal. Your first sentence must grab the readers, or they'll probably skip the whole section.

As in the case of newspaper articles, text is written in an inverted pyramid style, which places important information at the beginning, the supporting content following. Word count should be around fifty per cent less than for conventional print publications. Web users are looking for information instantly, so you need to get your point across in a concise and non-flowery way.

Bullet points

This is a clear way to point up vital information by splitting content into fast-read snippets. They give the page the required 'white space' for quick-scan reading.

Fees

Sometimes it's hard to tell a website's country of origin at first glance. If you are selling work to online markets based overseas, bear in mind that you will be paid in their currency, and that fees may sound more generous than when specified in pounds. Remember, a proportion of your fee will go in bank charges to convert the cheque into sterling, so it's a good idea to ask if they pay via an online banking service, such as PayPal.

Headings and subheadings

These act as content maps. Breaking up the text with headings means the reader can easily skim the page for the required information.

Highlighted keywords

Making certain words stand out from the rest draws the reader in and leads them quickly to vital information. This is achieved by using a different colour or emboldening key words, but don't overdo it, or it can make reading the text confusing.

Sending queries

The same level of care should be taken when querying by email, whether for an online or print publication, as in the case of a normal query letter.

- Set up an email address specifically for your writing submissions and use your real name in full as part of the address. This looks more professional than sending mail as diggerjim5 or catwoman123.
- Save a copy of your emails, so that you have a record

of what was written in each query, when it was sent, and to whom.

- In the subject line, type the word 'Query', followed by a three- or four-word description of your piece.
- Include full contact information, and succinct details of your query.
- List relevant credentials.
- Say where you have had similar work published. You could provide a link to your own website or to another website where a sample of your work is displayed. As not all editors will want, or have time, to visit these sites, always provide this information within the email, too.
- Don't send writing samples as an attachment.

Editors often respond more quickly to a query sent via email, but you should never assume that they will. The response time may still be several weeks, so if you hear nothing, leave it a month before sending a follow-up email.

Submitting the manuscript

If you have been given the go-ahead to submit your work by email, include the words 'Article submission', followed by the title, in the subject line. The editor will recognise this as something she is expecting and deal with it sooner than a piece sent in 'on spec'.

- If you are sending sidebar information, include this with the main article, rather than sending two separate attachments.
- Large graphic files can take a long time to download, so always seek permission before sending photographs by email.

Some editors will ask that you copy your work into the body of the email. The writers' guidelines will usually specify if the publication accepts attachments and in which format. Many publications prefer MS Word DOC and others will request work saved as plain text or a rich text format.

If you write in MS Word DOC format, you can save your submission as rich text without many problems. Saving the file as plain text will mean you lose any italics, and bold formatting. The recognised procedure is to use an asterisk either side of the word, or words, in your manuscript that you wish to appear in bold, like this: *bold*. To indicate where italics should appear, use an underscore either side of the word, or words, like this: _italic_.

To summarise:

- Keep paragraphs short and make one point per paragraph
- Use the inverted pyramid style of important information first
- Write web articles fifty per cent shorter than their print equivalent
- Use online formatting like highlighting, headings and bullet points
- Be professional when submitting queries and manuscripts via email
- Check the countries of origin to decide the viability of selling to them

Writers' Groups
See also: Feedback

Every week, many hundreds of writers' circles meet in venues around the UK, and even more writers take advantage of online writing groups. Most would agree they benefit from belonging to a group, but how exactly do they help?

Writing can be a lonely occupation – the original thought process, fact gathering, and researching markets, not to mention the actual creative bit and the agonies of the submission and rejection game. Writers profit from a supportive atmosphere, which helps them gain self-confidence to continue writing, or to submit work for publication. It's good to test out stories, articles, or book extracts on fellow writers. Spelling and grammatical errors are spotted and suggestions for improvement are often helpful.

Local

Some writers' groups are more ambitious than others. If you are serious about being published, choose a group that actively encourages this. Many produce anthologies of members' work and the way in which these are produced can say a lot about the general standard and experience of the group. The best groups are a mixture of published and unpublished writers – a group where everyone is unpublished may lack direction.

Activities include such things as:

- Reading your work to the group
- Offering criticism to other members
- Group writing exercises
- Competitions and writing related news
- Guest speakers
- Most local groups meet bi-weekly or monthly. The majority allow potential members to sit in on a couple of sessions before joining. This is useful for gauging whether your particular interests are covered adequately, and that you are not the only poet among prose writers, or vice versa.

Online

The Internet has provided a great way to meet other writers around the world through web-based writers' groups. As well as showcasing your work, mixing with others who have similar writing ambitions offers opportunities to network, sharing information on competitions, writing markets, and trends worldwide.

Although some writers prefer a local group that meets in person, an online writing group has many benefits.

- It can be less embarrassing to have others read your work from the screen, than reading it aloud to a group of people
- Online groups are available to everyone, no matter where they live
- There are no time restrictions – members can drop in anytime
- Members of online groups often have more time to read and offer in-depth comment than they might in a once-a-month meeting

Online writing groups are larger than local writers' circles and, by their nature, can be more impersonal and less 'hands-on'. But groups in both categories offer writers of all abilities mutual support and encouragement, whether they write as a hobby, or for publication.

To summarise:

- All writers profit from a supportive atmosphere
- Groups are excellent for testing out work on fellow writers
- If your aim is publication, choose a group that encourages this
- Local writers' circles generally allow free taster sessions

- Online groups are larger, but have no time limitations

Word Count

See also: Computers, Guidelines, Publishers

Keep your manuscript within a specified word count for the best possible chance of acceptance.

Short stories and non-fiction articles have to be written to a certain length, so that they fit the magazine's page layout. As a guide, a 1,000-word short story will fit on a single page. Editors know how many articles and stories will fill their magazines and will not be interested in pieces which don't conform to their carefully worked out system.

Always refer to the magazine's guidelines with regard to word count. Most editors allow a very small amount of leeway but try to write as close to the required number of words as possible. When writing the word count on the title page, round the figure up or down to the nearest ten.

Competition judges have to be more precise, and entries will be disqualified if they contain more words, or more lines of poetry, than the rules stipulate. Unless the rules state otherwise, always assume that the title should be included as part of the word count.

Books:

Shouldn't a novel be as long as it takes to tell the story? Why the need to write to a certain length? While book lengths need not be as exact as short stories and articles, you should still give some thought to the finished manuscript. The reason is a financial one; the costs of manufacturing a book, and the estimated sales, have a direct bearing on the length of a book.

If a book is much shorter than others competing in the

same market, the cover price will need to be set too low to justify the cost of producing it. And if it is much longer than competing books, it may have to be priced too high, and therefore not sell in sufficient quantity. This is especially true of works by unknown authors.

Some genre series – westerns, for example – can be as few as 45,000 words. The average length of a novel is between 75,000 and 95,000 words. Sagas and fantasy novels are often longer, but it would be rare indeed for a new novelist to get a book deal if it exceeded 150,000 words.

Children's series books, aimed at the younger reader, bridge the gap between picture books and chapter books and weigh in at between 1,000 and 6,000 words, depending on the publisher. Children's stand-alone fiction, again depending on the publisher, will be written to between 12,000 and 40,000 words. The average teen novel is anywhere from 30,000 to 45,000 words.

Counting the number of words in a manuscript is easy if you use your computer's word count facility and this figure is acceptable to most publishers.

But, editorially speaking, a manuscript's 'word count' equates to the amount of space the words will take up on the final printed page, rather than an exact word count. This average figure will depend on the font style used; for example, Courier New, set at 12 point, will give a vastly different count to 12 point Times New Roman.

But, if you are asked to supply this average figure, rather than the one your word processor produces, here's one way of calculating it:

1.   Take a random page from your manuscript and count the words in ten lines
2.   Divide this number by ten
3.   Count how many lines there are on a full page

4. Multiply these two figures and round up to a whole number

5. Multiply this by the number of pages in your manuscript

To summarise:

- Story and article length must conform to a magazine's page layout
- Publishers usually expect books to fall within set word counts
- An average figure, or an automatic word count, are acceptable to most publishers

X

The X Factor

See also: Books, Nom de Plume, Originality, Publishers, Synopsis

What is this mysterious X Factor – the thing that makes the difference between an average writer and a great one, or between a good book and a bestseller?

Every manuscript has to have something which makes it stand out from the rest. The first hurdle is to ensure it adheres to all the rules of good writing. Assuming it passes the presentation test, what else does it need?

Imagine yourself as the editor who has the mile-high slush pile. How many diaries of 30-something singletons, or books about hidden codes, or boy wizards, will you want to read? It is almost certain you'd soon reach breaking point, having had your fill of authors claiming to be the next Helen Fielding, Dan Brown, or JK Rowling. You'd be on the lookout for something new.

Don't just imitate what's gone before. Be original. Think in a different way to everyone else. Introduce new twists to old themes. Give your work the stamp of individuality. It is often said that publishers don't know what they're looking for until they find it, but that they can spot a book they want to publish within the first few pages.

So, for the publisher, the X Factor will be a new voice and a fresh perspective. And, as well as great writing, he will want to know who the book will appeal to, what it offers that is different, and how it can be marketed.

A title that captures the imagination, and a chapter opening that is unusual, intriguing, and hits the ground running, will go a long way towards making a good first impression.

To summarise:

- Learn the craft of writing well
- Be original – don't imitate other writers
- Intrigue the publisher by your opening lines

Y

Yours Sincerely – Examples of Letters

See also: *Agents, Books, Covering Letters, Editors, Envelopes and sae, Letterheads, Queries*

Keep the letter simple, clear and to the point. Sell yourself and your work in such a way that the recipients will know they are dealing with a professional.

Agent

Sample letter to an agent:

Dear (address the agent by name – call first and find out which agent deals with your type of material),

I have read on your website that you handle children's fiction. I have enclosed a synopsis and the first three chapters of my children's novel, *Vlad the Inhaler*. (If the guidelines say send only a synopsis, don't send chapters as well.) Vlad is a half-human vampire who doesn't know how to turn into a bat, suffers from asthma, is scared of the dark, and a vegetarian. As if that wasn't bad enough, his wicked family want to kill him. This is a dark, but humorous, novel aimed at 8-12-year-olds. The completed work of 45,000 words is the first part of a trilogy. I am currently working on the second book.

(In this paragraph give your writing background – if no published credits, leave this paragraph out, unless you can add something to give gravitas to your submission.)

I have enclosed a stamped addressed envelope for your reply; the manuscript is disposable.

Thank you for your time and I look forward to hearing from you.

Yours sincerely,
Lorraine Mace

Editor
Sample letter to a fiction editor:
Dear (use the editor's name),

Enclosed for your consideration is a disposable copy of my 1,000-word short story, *Jack's Ripper*. I have written fiction for (list credits if any – if none, leave this sentence out).

I enclose a stamped addressed envelope for your convenience.

Yours sincerely,
I. Wannawrite

Sample letter to a features editor:
Dear (find out editor's name – don't put Features Editor or Editor),

Would you be interested in a 1,200-word feature, *The Butcher's Hook*, a light-hearted look at real-life murderers who have disposed of their victims by putting food on the table? The article covers ten famous felons, all of whom had fingers in several pies.

An outline of the proposed feature is enclosed.

I have written for various publications including (here you list the most prestigious magazines and newspapers where your work has appeared. If you have not yet had any success, don't say so, just leave this paragraph out of the letter) and have attached some recent clips.

I look forward to hearing from you and have enclosed a stamped addressed envelope for your reply.

Yours sincerely,
A. Goodwriter

Publisher

Sample letter to a publisher of non-fiction books:

Dear (include both title and name of publisher),

Would you consider commissioning a book on (insert your subject matter), which I feel would fit your list? Research has shown there is a gap in the market that *your title* would fill. The market is crowded with books (on your subject), but *your title* is (state how it differs, or is better).

In this paragraph, you spell out your qualifications for being the best person to write the book and give a brief overview of who your target market would be.

Next give your writing credentials to show you have the ability and experience to write the book.

Attached is a full proposal (comprising synopsis, market information and chapter breakdown) and sample chapters. I estimate the completed length of *your title* to be x words. The completed manuscript would be available by (whatever date you feel is comfortably within your capability).

I look forward to hearing from you and have enclosed a stamped addressed envelope for your reply.

Yours sincerely,
A Hopeful Author

Sample letter to publisher of fiction:

Dear (address by full name),

I have enclosed a synopsis and the first three chapters of my children's novel, *Vlad the Inhaler*. Vlad is a half-human vampire who doesn't know how to turn into a bat, suffers from asthma, is scared of the dark, and a vegetarian. As if that wasn't bad enough, his wicked family want to kill him. This is a dark, but humorous, novel aimed at 8-12-year-olds. The completed work of 45,000 words is the first part of a trilogy. I am currently working on the second book.

This book would fit into your list (state where, this shows you have done your homework).

In this paragraph give your writing background – if you do not have any published credits, you should leave this paragraph out.

The manuscript is disposable and I have enclosed a stamped addressed envelope for your reply.

Yours sincerely,
Lorraine Mace

Z

ZZZZ – Sleep on It

See also: *Consistency, Continuity, Discipline – Staying on Topic, Final Checks, Professionalism*

One of the best weapons in your armoury for presenting professional work is time. Putting your writing away, out of sight and out of mind, for at least two weeks, enables you to come back to it having a fresh approach.

You will be amazed, and most probably horrified, at the errors, poor writing and general sloppiness contained in something you had thought a work of art. It is only after the writing has disappeared from your conscious mind completely that you can do justice to the editing process. The human brain is amazingly good at reading what it thinks should be on the page, rather than what is actually there.

Very often, you will only have one chance to impress an editor, so it is too important to risk messing up that opportunity, just because you are too keen to get the work in an envelope and sent on its way.

What to look for with fresh eyes and mind

- Spelling errors and typos – often of the most basic kind
- Missing, or misplaced, words
- Entire sentences not making sense because of cutting and pasting
- Muddled thought processes, so that the work as a whole doesn't say what you'd hoped
- Ideas not flowing logically from one aspect to the next

You may also find that the time away from the piece in question gives you a different view of how it should be treated. Sometimes a completely rewritten story, or article, is stronger and more vibrant than the original, but do remember to treat it as a new piece of work and, when you've finished, zzzz – sleep on it, before you submit it anywhere.

Additional Information

The following sections outline some useful reading matter, details of prizes, writers' associations, and general information of benefit to new writers.

What Happens If a Publisher Shows Interest?

You've received the phone call, email or letter that makes you jump for joy – a publisher is interested in your proposal. Once you come down from the ceiling you'll need to know what happens next. The following will give you some idea of what to expect, although the experience varies greatly from one publishing house to another.

From the moment you receive a positive response it would be a good idea to join the Society of Authors. They offer a contract vetting service at no charge for their members. The minefield of working through the various clauses in a publishing contract is not for the uninitiated – or faint-hearted.

Independent publishers

Very often, you will deal directly with the person at the top and a decision will come fairly quickly.

Because independents carry few staff members, much of the work is out-sourced. There are both benefits and drawbacks to this.

The decision making process which precedes an offer in a larger publishing house (see below) normally irons out any potential conflicts before they arise, but in a smaller house, because all views are not taken into account upfront, sometimes later input can cause problems.

The advantage of being able to work closely with the

publisher, being able to discuss your project as and when needed, offsets the drawbacks outlined above.

Larger publishing houses

The process in larger houses varies, but convincing the acquisitions editor is the first step in most houses. If the editor likes the idea it will be put before an editorial board who will say a provisional yes or definite no.

The next stage is for the editor to work out the costings. Production costs include editing, typesetting, design, proofreading, cover art and copywriting. From these projections and estimated potential sales the author's advance will be calculated. The figures will then be presented at a second editorial board meeting, where a final decision will be made whether or not to take the author on.

And then:

The advance is normally paid in stages and can be split into two – part on signing of contract, part on delivery of manuscript, or into three – a quarter on signing, half on delivery, and the remaining quarter on publication, or thirds at each of those stages.

The manuscript undergoes several phases before it appears as a book ready for your eager public to buy. The first of these is after typesetting, when a copy is sent to the author to correct any errors not picked up earlier, or that have occurred as a result of the typesetting. These changes are made without cost to the author. Any alterations after this point may be charged to the author.

For a non-fiction book, an index is created at proof stage (see Indexing).

Don't think your job was complete when you wrote 'The End' on your work of art. In today's tight marketing world, it was only the beginning, as your input will be required when it comes to promoting your book. The publisher has responsibility for getting the book into shops and other retail outlets, including listing the book in its catalogue. It is likely that promotional materials, such as news releases and flyers, will be distributed. Review copies will be sent out to everyone on the PR list, to which the author should have contributed.

After that, unless you are lucky enough to be a big name, very little promotional work is done by the publisher. This means that you, as the author, should be looking at ways of promoting your book and, indeed, should have outlined marketing ideas in your original proposal.

The success of your book will depend on how hard you work to promote it.

Series books

A book forming part of an existing series is the most straightforward. The books are written to a pre-determined format, having an exact word count and style spelled out, often at the proposal stage. The advance and contract conditions are standard for all authors and there is little to negotiate apart from submission and publication date.

The publisher normally provides an author guide, which covers such things as word count, style of writing, chapter layout, additional information required (lists of trivia and facts, for example), whether a foreword is required, if page numbering and/or indexing is needed, file formats to use if sent by email or on disk, page formatting if sent as hard copy, and when it needs the author's photo and biography for pre-launch publicity.

In short, everything you need to know is outlined for you from the moment the publisher says yes to your proposal.

Addresses

Arvon Foundation
Residential writing courses in four different locations around the UK.
The Arvon Foundation, 42a Buckingham Palace Road, London SW1W 0RE
Tel: 020 7931 7611
www.arvonfoundation.org

Authors' Licensing and Collecting Society Limited (ALCS)
Protects and promotes authors' rights.
The Writers' House, 13 Haydon Street, London EC3N 1DB
Tel: 020 7264 5700
www.alcs.co.uk

The Copyright Licensing Agency (CLA)
Information on copyright issues.
Saffron House, 6-10 Kirby Street, London EC1N 8TS
Tel: 020 7400 3100
www.cla.co.uk

Directory of Writers' Circles
Courses and workshops for writers.
39 Lincoln Way, Harlington, Beds LU5 6NG
www.writers-circles.com

The National Association of Writers' Groups
List of affiliated writers' groups, competitions and news for fiction and non-fiction writers, playwrights, poets and novelists.
The Arts Centre, Biddick Lane, Washington, Tyne & Wear NE38 2AB
www.nawg.co.uk

The Society of Authors
Guides for writers and news of grants, awards and prizes.
84 Drayton Gardens, London SW10 9SB
Tel: 020 7373 6642
www.societyofauthors.org

The Society of Indexers
Information on indexing and how to find an indexer.
Woodbourn Business Centre, 10 Jessell Street, Sheffield S9 3HY
Tel: 0114 244 9561
www.indexers.org.uk

The Writers Bureau
Offers a range of home-study courses.
Sevendale House, 7 Dale Street, Manchester M1 1JB
Tel: 0845 345 5995
www.writersbureau.com

The Writers' Guild of Great Britain
The trade union working on behalf of writers including guidance on rates of pay.
The Writers' Guild of Great Britain, 15 Britannia Street, London WC1X 9JN
Tel: 020 7833 0777
www.writersguild.org.uk

Awards and Prizes

The Asham Award
A biennial short story prize for new UK women writers over the age of 18.
Carole Buchan, Lewes Town Hall, High Street, Lewes, East Sussex BN7 2QS
Tel: 01273 483159
www.ashamaward.com

The Betty Trask Award
For romantic or traditional first novels, published or unpublished, by authors under the age of 35.
Awards Secretary, The Society of Authors, 84 Drayton Gardens, London SW10 9SB
Tel: 020 7373 6642
www.societyofauthors.org

The Bridport Prize
An annual creative writing competition for unpublished poetry and short stories.
Bridport Prize, Bridport Arts Centre, South Street, Bridport, Dorset DT6 3NR
www.bridportprize.org.uk

Crime Writers' Association Debut Dagger
Annual competition to find new crime writers.
PO Box 273, Boreham Wood, Hertfordshire WD6 2XA
www.thecwa.co.uk/daggers/debut/howtoenter.html

The Fish Prize
International awards for short stories and poetry.
Fish Publishing, Durrus, Bantry, Co. Cork, Ireland
www.fishpublishing.com/index.php

Jacqui Bennett Writers Bureau Competitions
Quarterly prizes for unpublished short stories and poetry.
Jenny Hewitt, Jacqui Bennett Writers Bureau, 87 Home

Orchard, Yate, South Gloucestershire BS37 5XH
Tel: 01454 324717
www.jbwb.co.uk
The McKitterick Prize
Annual prize for first published novels or unpublished typescripts by authors over the age of 40.
Awards Secretary, The Society of Authors, 84 Drayton Gardens, London SW10 9SB
Tel: 020 7373 6642
www.societyofauthors.org
The V S Pritchard Memorial Prize
Annual prize for an unpublished short story.
The Royal Society of Literature, Somerset House, Strand, London WC2R 1LA
Tel: 020 7845 4676
www.rslit.org
Write a Story for Children Competition
Annual prizes awarded to amateur writers over the age of 18.
ACW, Competition Entry, PO Box 95, Huntingdon, Cambridgeshire PE28 5RL
Tel: 01487 832752
www.childrens-writers.co.uk

Recommended Reading List

Eats, Shoots and Leaves by Lynne Truss (Gotham Books)

How to Write a Pantomime by Lesley Cookman (Accent Press)

How to Write and Sell Short Stories by Della Galton (Accent Press)

How to Write for Children – and get published by Louise Jordan (Piatkus
Books)

How to Write Travel Articles – In One Weekend by Diana Cambridge (Canal Street Publishing)

On Writing by Stephen King (New English Library)

Self-Editing for Fiction Writers by Renni Browne and Dave King (Harper Paperbacks)

Successful Article Writing by Gillian Thornton (Thomas & Lochar)

Successful Novel Plotting by Jean Saunders (Accent Press)

Wannabe a Writer? by Jane Wenham-Jones (Accent Press)

What If? Writing Exercises for Fiction Writers by Anne Bernays and Pamela Painter (HarperCollins Publishers)

Writing a Play by Steve Gooch (A & C Black Publishers Ltd)

Resources for writers

Books

Children's Writers' & Artists' Yearbook
A directory for children's writers and artists, published by A&C Black Ltd
Writers' & Artists' Yearbook
Expert advice, writing tips and resources, published by A&C Black Ltd
www.writersandartists.co.uk
The Writer's Handbook
A guide for all writers, containing market listings, published by Macmillan

Magazines

Freelance Market News
Monthly guide to writing markets.
Angela Cox, The Association of Freelance Writers,
Sevendale House, 7 Dale Street, Manchester M1 1JB
Tel: 0161 228 2362
www.freelancemarketnews.com
Mslexia
Advice, news, interviews, competitions, events, courses and grants.
Mslexia Publications Limited, PO Box 656, Newcastle upon Tyne NE99 1PZ
Tel: 0191 261 6656
www.mslexia.co.uk
The New Writer
Prizes for unpublished fiction, poetry, essays and articles.
The New Writer, PO Box 60, Cranbrook, Kent TN17 2ZR
Tel: 01580 212626

www.thenewwriter.com

Writers' Forum

A magazine for writers of short stories, magazine features, novels, plays, film scripts and poetry.

Writers' Forum, PO Box 6337, Bournemouth BH1 9EH

Tel: 0120 258 6848

www.writers-forum.com

Writers' News and Writing Magazine

Advice, market listings, interviews and competitions.

Writers' News and Writing Magazine, 5th Floor, 31-32 Park Row, Leeds LS15JD

Tel: 0113 200 2929

www.writersnews.co.uk

Websites

BBC Writers Room

Encourages script writing talent and includes details of writing events, opportunities and news.

BBC writersroom, 1st Floor, Grafton House, 379-381 Euston Road, London NW1 3AU

www.bbc.co.uk/writersroom

Bibliomania

Free online resource covering reference books, fiction, non-fiction, biographies, poetry and drama.

www.bibliomania.com

Booktrust

Information on the publishing industry, literary prizes and book awards, and fact-sheets for writers.

Book House, 45 East Hill, London SW18 2QZ

Tel: 020 8516 2977

www.booktrust.org.uk

The British Library

A vast collection including books, manuscripts, maps, newspapers, magazines, patents, prints and drawings, music scores and photographs.

96 Euston Road, London NW1 2DB
www.bl.uk

My Writers Circle

A forum and resource for both beginners and advanced writers.

www.mywriterscircle.com

Online English Grammar

Help with the use of punctuation and writing good English.

www.edufind.com/english/grammar/index.cfm

PlaysOnTheNet

News and information for playwrights. Theatre database.

www.playsonthenet.com/potn/

Romantic Novelists' Association

Includes a new writers' scheme for unpublished authors.

www.rna-uk.org

Story

The campaign that celebrates the short story including news, projects and competitions.

www.theshortstory.org.uk

The Word Pool

Articles, reviews and information on writing for children.

www.wordpool.co.uk

Writelink

Online community of new and published writers including resources, news and competitions.

www.writelink.co.uk

WritersServices

Information and resources for new, and published, authors.

www.WritersServices.com

YouWriteOn

Website sponsored by the Arts Council of England.
www.youwriteon.com

Glossary of Useful Terms

AA: author alteration

AC: author corrections

Advance: money paid to the writer against future royalties

Advanced copies: books sent out by printer or publisher before publication date

AI: advance information used in the marketing of books

Appendix/ces: additional information, usually at end of book

Auctions: held by an agent if two or more publishers express interest in a book

Backlist: books that continue to sell steadily over a long period of time

Blind folio: an unprinted page

Blurb: a short description of a book and/or author on a book jacket

Body text: main text of a document

Bullet: a large dot preceding text

Caps: an abbreviation for capital letters

Caption: text identifying a picture or illustration

Catch line: a temporary headline or title

Character count: the number of characters in a piece of text, which includes all letters, figures, signs or spaces

Copy: text

Copyright: protection given to the creator of work to prevent unauthorised use

Dagger and double dagger: reference marks for footnotes

Earning out: selling enough copies of a book to cover the advance

End pages: material after the main text

Extent: page count in a book

Flush left: copy aligned to left margin

Flush right: copy aligned to right margin

Foldout/Gatefold: a sheet of paper folded into the book for a map or chart

Foreword: an endorsement of the book and/or author

Folio: page number

Galley proof: copy of text for checking before print run

Ghost-writing: writing a book for which someone else will take the credit

Gutter: the inside margins toward the binding edge

Hard copy: printed document

House style: rules for spelling, punctuation and grammar used in a publishing house or magazine

Imprint (1): the publisher's or printer's details given in a book

Imprint (2): over print on a previously printed page

ISBN: International Standard Book Number

Justify: alignment of text with both margins

Loose leaf: binding allowing the insertion and removal of pages

Manuscript (ms): a hand or typewritten document

Margins: non-printing areas at top, bottom and sides of page

Mark up: text showing typesetting instructions

Masthead: publisher's details, as found on magazines and newspapers

Mid-list: books which are not by big name or celebrity authors

Option: when a publisher asks for first sight of your next work

Page count: total number of pages including blank pages

Page proof: stage following galley proofs

Pagination: the numbering of pages

PE: printer error

POD: print (or publishing) on demand

Prelim pages: the pages at the start of a book before the main text including the title page, copyright notice, dedications, foreword, contents and list of illustrations

Print run: number of books printed in one job

Proof reading marks: a standard set of symbols used to indicate corrections on proofs

Proof: a copy for checking

Public Lending Right: annual payment to registered authors when their books are borrowed from public libraries

Reference marks: symbols in text linked to a footnote or endnote

Reprint: a reprint of an article previously published in a magazine

Remainders: unsold books

RRP: Recommended Retail Price

Script: the dialogue and instructions for a play or film

Slush pile: slang expression for unsolicited submissions

Small caps: capital letters of equal size type to the lower case letters

Small presses: independent (usually literary) magazines

Spread: open page size of a book

STM: scientific, technical and medical

Stet: proof correction meaning let the original copy stand

Subscript: small characters set below normal text

Superscript: small characters set above normal text

TIFF (Tagged Image File Format): format for digital information

Trade publishing: term used for publishing intended for the general consumer market

Transparency: slide photograph

Typescript: a typed manuscript
Typo: typographical error
uc/lc: upper/lower case
UCC: Universal Copyright Convention
wf: mark up on manuscript meaning wrong font

More titles in the
Secrets to Success Writing Series
from Accent Press...

Love Writing – How to Make Money Writing Romantic or Erotic Fiction

Sue Moorcroft

Love sells and sex sells and you can earn your living writing about them in novels, novellas and short stories as well as serials for magazines, anthologies and websites.

This book holds the secrets of how to achieve success.

As well as drawing on her experience as a fiction writer and creative writing tutor, in this 'must-have' book Sue has included questions from aspiring writers – with illuminating responses from published writers and industry experts.

Romantic fiction encompasses everything from chart-topping chick lit and romantic comedies, through gritty sagas, sweeping historicals and smouldering erotica to liver-twisting affairs with vampires. Bright, emotional, involving, intelligent storytelling about love and desire is what readers want and will pay for.

Do you want to know how to create emotional punch? (Or even what emotional punch *is?*) How to control dual time lines? Spring your work out of the slush pile? Write a tender love scene that excites passion rather than hilarity? This book reveals all.

ISBN 9781906373993 price £9.99

Wannabe a Writer?

Jane Wenham-Jones
Foreword by Katie Fforde

This hilarious, informative guide to getting into print is a must-have for anyone who's ever thought they've got a book in them.

Drawing on her own experiences as a novelist and journalist, **Writing Magazine's** agony aunt **Jane Wenham-Jones** takes you through the minefield of the writing process, giving advice on everything from how to avoid Writers' Bottom to what to wear to your launch party.

Including hot tips from authors, agents and publishers at the sharp end of the industry, **Wannabe a Writer?** tells you everything you ever wanted to know about the book world – and a few things you didn't...

Contributors include writers Frederick Forsyth, Ian Rankin, Jilly Cooper and Jill Mansell and publishers Harper Collins, Hodder Headline and Simon & Schuster as well as leading journalists and agents.

www.wannabeawriter.co.uk

ISBN 9781905170814 price £9.99

Successful Novel Plotting

Jean Saunders

**Lost the plot? Get help with this invaluable writers' guide
and in no time you'll be turning out
real page-turners.**

What is it about a good book that hooks the reader and makes them want more? *A good plot.*

Every best-selling author from Agatha Christie to Terry Pratchett knows the importance of a strong story.
But for the budding author it can be daunting and even confusing.

How do you turn that seed of an idea into a great epic?

This authoritative guide will help steer new writers through the minefield of the writing process.

Using examples from her own work, and that of other top authors, Jean explains how to create memorable characters, generate cliff-hangers and keep up a pace that will hook readers.

Jean Saunders is an award-winning author of more than 600 short stories and 100 novels. She's best-known as Rowena Summers, the writer of many novels based in the West Country, and Rachel Moore, author of wartime sagas set in Cornwall. Her WW1 saga Bannister Girls was short-listed for the Romantic Novel of the Year award. Jean now lectures on writing and writes a monthly column for Writing Magazine.

ISBN 978190637627 price £9.99.